THE PRINTER'S DEVIL

A MAGAZINE OF NEW WRITING

Edited by
Stephen Plaice, Sean O'Brien
and Eva Salzman

First published in England 1994 by
The Printer's Devil
Top Offices
13a Western Road
Hove BN3 1AE
Tel/Fax 0273 720894

ISBN 1 85242 061 8

Editorial Board
Stephen Plaice   Sean O'Brien
Terry James   Eva Salzman
Don Paterson   Sue Roe
Fiachra Gibbons   Nicky Singer

Publicity
Polly Marshall

Administration
Sue Stevens

Trade distribution by
Serpent's Tail   4 Blackstock Mews   London N4 2BT
Tel: 071 345 1949   Fax: 071 704 6467

Electronic layout by
Vicky Sharman
118 Richmond Road Brighton

Printed by
Andy Wilson Associates
19 Elder Place Brighton

End of England

THE DEVIL'S CONFESSIONAL

NICK HORNBY	Envy	12
MICHAEL DONAGHY	Irena of Alexandria	18
CAROLE COATES	Clever	19
ALISON SPRITZLER-ROSE	Penis Envy	29

THE DEVIL'S SERMON — 30

FIACHRA GIBBONS	Sorry for your Troubles	33
EVA SALZMAN	A Class Act	40
STEPHEN PLAICE	Something Blue	45
PETER ARMSTRONG	A Postcard of the Market-Place	52
KEN SMITH	Visiting the Dead	54
SEAN O'BRIEN	On the Road Again	63
U. A. FANTHORPE	The Silence	66

THE DEVIL'S AUDIENCE with U. A. Fanthorpe — 68

EMILIA DI GIROLAMO	The Spell	93
SOPHIE HANNAH	Masks	101
	The Zookeeper	103
FRED D'AGUIAR	Towards Home	105
LES MURRAY	Contested Landscape at Forsayth	112
RUTH PADEL	Tell Me About It	114
PAUL EUSTICE	Six Eggs	116

End of England

EDITORIAL

THIS IS the End of England. The country is no longer By Appointment to the Royal Household. The Devil is a citizen, not a subject. This issue hopes to accelerate the Republic. Despite popular demand, the Devil will not seek nomination as its President. It would be hell.

We identify Envy as the prevalent deadly sin at the End of England. The Devil has certainly envied Nick Hornby since the publication of *Fever Pitch*. But who have the envied envied?

No one has complained that we do not bring enough news from the Shires. But to preempt No one's complaint, the Devil journeyed west to the Cotswolds to interview U. A. Fanthorpe, the first woman to be nominated for the Oxford Chair of Poetry. Oxford stood by its policy of one vote, one man.

The Devil was unable to vote, too busy canvassing for The Society of the Suppression of Virtue. On his travels, he was heartened to discover that witchcraft is thriving in Buckinghamshire. What else is there to do on a council estate these days? The Old Religion is pushing up through the cracks in the concrete. Emilia Di Girolamo reports.

Ken Smith brings an exclusive from the dead, who are now

EDITORIAL

sleeping rough as a result of Care in the Community.

Enoch Powell declined to give the Devil a piece on immigration. But Fred D'Aguiar obliged. We also review the Criminal Justice Bill in this last issue before the Devil's Masses (editorial meetings) are deemed a threat to public order, and made illegal. So no more live poultry through the post please.

In anticipation of the fall of the Monarchy, the Devil would be pleased to receive Anthems or Battle Hymns of the Republic. Special consideration will be given to entries from Manchester.

See you in the Tower.

THE DEVIL'S INDEX now includes:

Supplicants who try to get matey with the Devil.

Letters inquiring after the Devil's maximum length. It depends who's asking.

Contributions with a Table of Contents. We do that.
Questionnaires and brochures from quangos purporting to develop audiences for literature. Get real.

Letters from non-subscribers requesting information. The Devil welcomes the new trend of cash for questions.

Among THE DEVIL'S POST:

from James D. Kenneally

'Enclosed you will find my poem Eire and Me, which I sincerely hope you will publish for two reasons:

A) This fine piece of literary execution possesses, surely, an innate capacity to grasp, most vehemently, the collective unconsciousness of a distressed generation.
B) I'm an egotistical bastard who needs to see his work in print before the next millennium.'

THE DEVIL'S CONFESSIONAL

DEADLY SIN: ENVY

NICK HORNBY

ENVY

BETWEEN THE ages of, I guess, twenty and thirty-odd, I envied the following people for varying lengths of time: my sister, who had a job that involved travel and glamour and expense claims (she once met Lady Di! She once met Michael Powell!); my sister's boyfriend, who had a job that involved travel and glamour and expense claims, and who had written a book; the teacher who taught in the classroom next to mine, whose lessons were orderly yet enriching, quiet but companionable, whereas mine were catastrophic and chaotic and frequently unpleasant; my friend Pete, who had his own flat, and trendy taps in bright primary colours; supporters of different football teams, teams that won things, and went to Wembley for Cup Finals; Roddy Doyle (I could have written that book *The Commitments*, if... if... if I'd been him); anyone who reviewed records; anyone who reviewed books; anyone who reviewed films; anyone who wrote films; anyone who wrote books; anyone who had ever met somebody famous that they admired; anyone who could afford to eat in a smart-looking Thai restaurant near Sadlers' Wells that I went past on the bus; anyone who worked in television; anyone who had ever met anyone who had written in *The Face*; anyone whose name had ever appeared in print, even in a fanzine or an in-house magazine; anyone who had ever had an interview after applying for a job they had seen advertised in *The Guardian* Media Page; anyone who knew something I didn't; anyone who had ever done anything at all.

There were some people that I did not envy. I did not envy any man I knew his girlfriend or wife, although occasionally I envied couples their children and bookcases and wine racks. I did not envy anybody a talent that I knew for sure I did not have, a generosity which thankfully allowed me to listen to music and go to football matches without a sudden attack of bile - I had long known that I couldn't sing or play sports very well, and I did not despise those that could. I did not envy anyone who had jobs which obliged them to work at weekends, or late at night, however much money they earned. And, of course, I did not envy anyone less fortunate than myself.

But that was it, really, as far as equanimity went. Most of the time I was envious. (I was so envious, in fact, that at one stage I was going to write a thriller about an arty serial killer who went round rubbing out people whose work was, in his estimation, inferior to his own. I thought that writing the book would be better for me than killing the people, but in the end I did neither, as far as I can remember.) I had a soundtrack for this envy, too: the first three or four Elvis Costello albums, which contained just the right amount of spite and sonic fury to alleviate the suffering. Like the persona Costello adopted, I told myself that I didn't want to go to Chelsea either, but of course I did, desperately.

There are, I guess, some people who are not motivated by envy, but I wasn't one of them. I wanted to do things because other people were doing them, and seemed to be having a good time doing them. There are some people - Joyce, say, or Beckett, or even Wodehouse, amongst writers, Hendrix, a lot of musicians, painters, poets - who you feel would have ended up doing what they did, even if they'd had to single-handedly invent their chosen medium. They couldn't help what they did. And though I did have ambitions for myself and my writing, many of the reasons I had for wanting to write were not noble ones. I did not want to travel to work, for example. I did not want to wear a suit. I did not want to have to suck up to people more important than myself. (I had no idea then that writers spend most of their time sucking up to people more important than themselves.) I wanted to be able to watch England internationals played on midweek afternoons. I wanted to play snooker with Martin and Julian on the days that the muse stubbornly and inexplicably refused to descend. (You know how it is, guys.) Being a writer, it seemed to me, would be like staying home sick from school every day of my life, except there would be nothing wrong with me, and nor would I have to pretend that there was. (Later, I would find out that these absurd daydreams were bang on. True, I haven't been invited to play snooker with Martin and Julian, but I have watched all the England internationals played on midweek afternoons.)

I have stopped being envious now - not because I have matured, or mellowed, or because I have examined my soul and sickened myself with what I saw there, but because I can eat in the Thai restaurant near Sadlers' Wells if I want (in fact, it's not that swanky, and I ended up disappointed) and I have seen my name in print. Last year I went to Leeds and stayed in a hotel which had a CD player in each room... *and the publishers paid!* This one night, I reckon, made up for all the others on its own. But my point is this: where would we be without this kind of envy? What's so wrong with it? How many films and records and books - great ones - would never get made if we all stoically accepted our lot, knuckled down and got on with things? What is the difference, in fact, between envy and ambition?

There is another kind of envy, a useless, sad, dreamy kind which you can't do anything with - the kind of envy which makes you desire things that are simply not within reach, no matter how talented you are, or hard you work, or lucky you get. Maybe not everyone feels this - maybe you have to have been born at a certain time, and brought up in a certain place, I don't know. But - lucky me - I was born in exactly the right time, and grew up in exactly the right place, or at least, that's what it feels like now. I have written about my childhood and schooldays elsewhere, but I wish to emphasise here just how grey was the Britain of my youth. We wore grey school uniforms, and went to single-sex schools, and were taught by middle-aged men who were content, for lesson after lesson after lesson, to dictate to us from notes they had prepared ten years earlier.

According to social history, life should have been anything but grey: I went to secondary school between Woodstock and punk, and therefore life had a soundtrack of Bowie and Bolan, Rod and Elton, Roxy and Queen - colourful people. But they just sat there on the TV screen. They didn't spill out, somehow, and in any case some of the other stuff that was going on - the three-day week, the frequent power cuts - tended to take the shine off the new glam Britain we could see on *Top of the Pops*. Sitting in candlelight, waiting for the primus to heat up the tins of tomato soup, listening to government ministers pleading with us not to hoard food, we had more in common with our parents and their wartime experiences than we did with Freddy Mercury. One could argue that at least my youth had an identity of its own - there have been many more anonymous seven-year periods in contemporary British life. But the summers didn't seem longer then, as they are supposed to when you get older; in fact, I can't remember there being a summer in the first half of the '70s.

I had nothing to compare any of this with until I started to teach, at the beginning of the '80s; that is when I began to get envious. Of course, life had in many ways become more difficult for teenagers in the intervening decade. Unemployment, harder drugs, increasing incidence of teenage pregnancy... that whole Grange Hill/Eastenders Social Issue scene seemed to have been invented since I had sat my 'A'-levels. But Britain had changed in other, better ways, too. I taught in a mixed-sex school, for example; there hadn't been one in my dormitory town. Boys and girls sat in the same classroom, talked to each other, went out together without attempting to grapple each other to the floor. Their school uniform consisted of jeans and sweatshirts; there were more colours in their hair than there had been in my entire teenage wardrobe.

They had discovered politics, too. To my generation, politics had been Heath and Wilson and Enoch Powell, stuff that clogged up the pre-sports section of the mid-evening news; to theirs, politics was CND and Two-Tone and vegetarianism and the Clash, loud single-issue rants that they understood, to their own satisfaction, at any rate, and which they cared about as much as we had cared about Morecambe and Wise. They knew what sexism was (we had barely grasped the rudimentary principles of sex); they knew what racism was (the Asian kids at our school had been subjected to shameful but entirely routine barracking). They were articulate, relaxed, funny, positive and peaceable (we were tongue-tied, uptight, and breathed in an atmosphere of barely-repressed violence) and more than anything, I wanted to start all over again. I didn't want to teach them. I wanted to be one of them.

I like to think that I have spent comparatively little time envying people their youth. I am glad that my record collection does not consist entirely of techno; I am glad too that I do not have a dog on a piece of string, and that I do not have to laugh uproariously at Vic Reeves, or examine in minute detail the lyric sheets of Pearl Jam albums. And in any case, I was young - twenty-five - when I started teaching, and I was therefore not yet aware that youth was worth envying. It wasn't their youth I was after, but their self-confidence and their self-respect and their sense of self-esteem; the '70s might have looked like the Me Decade to Tom Wolfe, but Mao's Red Guard had been allowed to retain more ego than the boys at Maidenhead Grammar School. I was also - and this could be the key to the whole thing, right here - desperately covetous of their ability to dance. *Young Guns Go For It* might have been a silly piece of teen fluff compared to, say, *Paranoid*, but there was no doubting which was easier to shake a leg to. And anyway, they all knew people they could dance with. At the dances I went to, asking someone to take to the floor was like waving a packet of Durex in her face; but to these kids, dancing was just dancing, and no big deal.

I thought that the people I taught would be famous by the mid-'90s, when they hit their late twenties. I thought they'd all be acting and writing and doing all kinds of stuff that I had never had the confidence to attempt when I was their age. But they're not - none of them have come to anything, yet. The people doing the acting and the writing and all kinds of stuff are, presumably, people like me, people who spent their twenties burnt up with rage and jealousy and resentment. So I don't envy them any more, because in the end, when the chips were down, they had something missing: the necessary degree of bile.

MICHAEL DONAGHY

IRENA OF ALEXANDRIA

Creator, thank You for humbling me.
Creator, who twice empowered me to change
a jackal to a saucer of milk,
a cloud of gnats into a chandelier,
and once, before the emperor's astrologers,
a nice distinction into an accordion,
and back again, thank You
for choosing Irena to eclipse me.

She changed a loaf of bread into a loaf of bread,
caused a river to flow downstream,
left the leper to limp home grinning and leprous,
because, the bishops say, Your will burns
bright about her as a flame about a wick.

Thank You, Creator, for taking the crowds away.
Not even the blind come here now.
I have one bowl, a stream too cold to squat in,
and the patience of a saint. Peace be,
in the meantime, upon her. And youth.
May sparrows continue to litter her shoulders,
children carpet her steps in lavender,
and may her martyrdom be beautiful and slow.

CAROLE COATES

CLEVER

BEING CLEVER together. That's what they had in their relationship from the beginning. Still have in its interminable or terminal stage now they've married. They don't tell anyone they're married. They still talk about 'my partner' as if legal heterosexuality was closure and they wanted to keep all their options open, at least verbally. They have short sensible names - John and Jean - unobtrusive. He might occasionally fiddle with a consonant or so on his headed notepaper. She doesn't bother. But he is a writer, after all. He can spell his name how he damn well likes.

They have a very good house - about which they have been, intermittently, apologetic. Less so now. John keeps the house extremely well. There are always fresh flowers in the same places: the big windows in the front, so that anyone who looks up from the street sees the tall stone house framing posy after posy.

Jean earns the money. John is the writer. Or Writer. He writes thrillers. He reads thrillers. He doesn't sell them much. But he will do. Probably. Maybe.

He knows, anyway, about the private dick. And his particular brands of sadness: the inevitable treacheries, the tough words, the gorgeous blonde going bad. He knows every fag-end of those mean streets. In the States anyway. Not here. Not in North Lancashire.

Jean reads his books. But Jean isn't a writer. She's busy. Clever but busy. Although she doesn't want to talk about it - he doesn't want to hear too much about it - she has a demanding, responsible job. And she is nice. She likes the bits of paper she pushes about on her desk. She is, but she mightn't like it said, efficient. And clever. That's why she likes John. They can be clever together. There are plenty of things and people to be clever together about. Her colleagues, for example.

She had us all round when she first took the job. Most of us were apprehensive, cagey. Not me. The rest gave so little away that the only theorising John and Jean could do was to say 'anal retentive'. But Jean's brisk competence and John's ferocious silences are a formidable combination, especially when John wears his baseball cap. Back to front.

I've never been diffident in my life. A chatty lady. Expressive even. And a poet. Chatty and a poet. And a drinker. This is a completely useless boast, but I used to hold my own, pint for pint, with a young man I lived with when pubs first stayed open for twelve hours a day. This was the sort of thing Jean and John liked. Not that they'd drink bitter. Too fattening. Maybe Coors. But certainly not Boddingtons.

What else did they like about me? A slightly raffish but familiar history of good old '60s sex and drugs, '70s adultery and politics, and all the complex, fracturing relationships of the '80s. It was close to John's story. I think. I don't know. He didn't go in for autobiography. Dark hints. The odd horror story. Crazy Salvation Army relatives in a rundown seaside town? Drugs and crack-ups and suicide wards? That and shagging some famous names of 1967.

At a certain time in the evening, fifth bottle time, I used to find myself in a 'who was most fucked up as a kid' competition with him. I always used to win because I like talking about myself. He wanted to be most fucked up, but could never bring himself to dish the details. More dark hints. Once, when Jean had crashed out on the sofa covered with cats, John had talked. It was tenth bottle time. I can remember watching the logs turn to ash and trying to remember a poem I'd written and lost when I was in Spalding and which may have had some good lines.

When I saw him a few days later, he was very formal.

'Rosamund, I feel I must apologise to you.'

He's tall and I had to peer up, surprised. People normally call me Rosie.

'I bored you to death the other night. You didn't want to hear all that stuff.'

'What stuff?'

'Tedious details about my ex-wife and the kids. My mother. Just forget about it. I was drunk.'

I was fascinated.

'You needn't worry. I was too pissed to take any of it in or remember it.'

'Bitch.'

And he walked off, furious, his leathers creaking.

It seemed like a good idea to get some people together. My plan was to organise regular meetings where people could read and discuss their writing - whatever it was - poems, short stories, plays or bits of novels. This town is full of groups like that. My particular spin on the idea was that it should include alcohol and a committed small group.

When I mentioned the plan to John and Jean, they suggested their house as venue. It was central and they had plenty of comfortable chairs and glasses. And not a lot of visitors.

John was enthusiastic. I did the contacting and the phoning and the photo-copying and Jean treated it as a useful and harmless interest for John. We soon had our serious group. Every second Thursday, we arrived with manuscript and bottle.

I suppose John found my poems fascinating because they are not even acceptably 'Contemporary', let alone 'Post-Modern'. Old-fashioned stuff with few cultural references - no recent films or cellphones or *Neighbours*. No mention of John Major. I never ever worked out what a 'double whammy' was.

'I - I - I - I,' erupted John. 'As if you really existed as a unitary subject - the old Romantic "I".'

'If you don't believe that, you can only write parody,' I said. 'Unless you pretend to be someone else. Can't I pretend to be myself?'

I had just read out a poem about an incident from my childhood. My violent father figured.

'Representative late twentieth century experience,' said John. 'Nothing unique. After all...'

'I experienced it uniquely.'

'It's other people's experience too. You're not the only person it happened to.'

'Well, if it happened to you, write about it - give the Detroit Mafia a rest.'

John looked about angrily. The others were silent. After six months they were becoming more silent.

Jean came down from her study like a Girl Guide doing a Merit badge.

Time to wind up the evening.

'Of course it is difficult when you haven't read a lot of American thrillers to really discuss your novel intelligently, John. I think we're bringing some very English assumptions to it,' Fran said, spreading brie on a crumbling digestive biscuit and waving Foucault away. He arched his back, tail up.

'Why don't you read some of your other novel - your English one - then?' said Jean. John glared at her.

'You're writing another?' we said.

It seemed that he was. It seemed that he always worked on three at a time.

'It doesn't do to get too involved,' he said, still glaring.

'But this one's set in England?' I asked. 'Not an American thriller?'

'It's local, but it's still a thriller. But a bit more exploratory than the others.'

He was very defensive.

'Autobiographical, then?' Jo said and laughed.

'Certainly not. I'm not hoodwinked by all that "discovering yourself" essentialist crap.'

Most of the others were, of course. The talk went on. The room suggested muted shades of all our lives. Camp '30s seaside china in the cabinet, but not too much; the stopped efficiency of the Victorian station clock; the clever comfort of the Heal's stool; really faded pot-pourri. The shared aesthetic was comforting. It meant that we would all spend the same sort of money in the same sort of shops. It probably unified us more than our writing.

When there wasn't anything to talk about - when Jean came in - we could talk about the cats. Jean had a mafia of cats. Foucault, Derrida, Gramsci and Baudrillard - two tabbies, a black, and a black and white. They would bang their way through the cat flap, one after another, tough, dependent and idiotic. Jean adored them. The evening was safe when the cats came in.

'I've got another tussle with the DSS tomorrow,' Phil said after reading a scene of dialogue set in a Claims office. 'Got to prove I'm still job hunting.'

'What are they like here?' I asked. 'I had problems just getting through the door in Manchester.'

'They're OK. Pretty efficient really.'

'They never did sort my claim out.'

'What the fuck do you mean?' exploded John from the other side of the room. 'If you were unemployed and you filled in the right form you would have got your Giro. It's as simple as that.'

'No. Not if you're a married woman, separated from your husband. There are problems. Insurance stamps, for example.'

He glared across at me, not seeing anyone else.

'It always gets back to you being a woman, doesn't it? A helpless female who has to depend on men. You can't even fill in a form by yourself.'

'For God's sake! I couldn't pay insurance stamps all the time I was having babies. I couldn't work then.'

'Why not? I'm still paying out money to my ex-wife because she decided she would just sit about on her arse.'

I tried to get the evening functioning again.

'The guy I saw there - a charmer - said something about a computer malfunctioning.'

This didn't help.

'Of course he would be charming. And aren't you charming with your female tact smoothing everything over?'

I ignored this. 'And he didn't seem to know much more about computers than I do.'

'No, you're far too sweetly female to know how to work a PC, aren't you?'

'The most empowering thing I ever did was learn to drive. Why don't you try it?'

He didn't answer.

Each Thursday became more of a strain for me. I saw the others sitting back and waiting for the John/Rosie floorshow to begin. I sensed their minor resentment. I began to feel I was turning into a 'case' for John and Jean. Why did my past seem to fascinate them so much? What had they been doing all their lives, I wondered - hanging themselves up in their good pine wardrobes after work every day?

My life at that time was altogether alarming. A huge almost Puccini-orchestrated relationship was dying in a melodramatic way. (I'd told Jean about it privately, but 'Try women next time' John had said when I saw him a few days later.)

The meetings became combative. I began to feel like the one in *Gladiators* who drops his pugil stick very early on. Except that I was never given one. Other people seemed exempt. But other people stopped coming. It was awkward. Jean was my boss, after all. But sometimes even she would lose her temper with him.

'You're always driving my friends away,' she said acidly, and a week later: 'We're talking about splitting up.'

A fortnight afterwards, he said 'We're going to get married', and then a week later: 'She's not as nice as she makes out, wait and see, she's a real bitch.'

Then, a few days later, grudgingly, from her: 'I suppose he looks after me well enough.'

After a year of Thursdays, I felt wary. What game was I in? I thought I would change the scenery. I invited them to The Jade Dragon. It was time I was the host.

It wasn't a success. Half the town had decided to eat Chinese that night. We were horribly crowded: other people seemed to be in the crook of our elbows; their knees under our table; their breath in our hair. We drank too much too quickly. We didn't want to be there.

John cringed at the noise. He was wearing an enormous black fedora. Behind it, Chinese faces loomed up from the tobacco smoke. We had ordered the Special. John looked at me.

'Time has run back at least twenty years. I never thought I'd see dungarees again.'

'Stop it,' said Jean. 'Can't you see they're silk?'

'Does that make it OK?'

'It makes it expensive,' I said.

'This whole town's stuck in the '70s. Why do you have to collude with it?'

'I'm old enough to wear what I like. And I like red silk dungarees.'

'You look like a Habitat deckchair.'

'1970s or '90s Habitat? Make sure your cultural references are specific.'

'A pity about the upper arms,' he said.

'Take your shirt off then,' I said. 'Let's see yours, you silly sod.'

John and Jean looked surprised. Politeness was getting too hard for any of us.

After a pause, he started to talk about his novel. Not *The Shopping Mall Murders*, but the other one, the one he hadn't been reading on Thursdays. The English one. There was a 'hero' of sorts - a passive middle-aged thriller writer who lodged with a middle-aged female poet in this, our home town. The description of the poet made me look up.

'It sounds like me.'

'No.'

'It does.'

'Her eyes are green. Yours aren't.'

25

'They're hazel. What are you up to?'
'There are a few minor resemblances - poet, female, age, same town - but it's hardly you.'
'Her recent past sounds familiar too. I want to see this. Have you read it?'
Jean looked thoughtful. 'Yes,' she said.
I backtracked a bit.
'Perhaps it's a compliment,' I said, but I didn't believe it.

That evening, John gave me six chapters of *First Person Singular* ('Sounds like an Alan Ayckbourn,' I said). I read them that night. Yes, he had used all my stuff, even parodying a couple of my poems. He described my house, my hair ('the wrong sort of blonde'), my past, my daughters. My ex-husband. The clothes were 'loose and baggy like her ideas'; she'd published in 'the little vegetarian magazines'. The latest relationship was presented in some detail and with familiar vocabulary (I particularly remember 'Puccini'). The relationship between the poet and thriller writer was whimsically combative. The setting was this town. The title page showed that he'd chosen yet another pseudonym for himself.

I had a mirror - round with an old soft-green fluted china surround and a gold rim. I had seen myself there year after year, and I was used to the particular configurations of the old glass and my face and the soft colours. It reminded me of my grandmother, although I'd got it from Oxfam. I lent my house to some friends with street-wise adolescent children. When I got back, everything had been put back to rights, but they hadn't noticed my mirror in the bedroom.

I looked for my face in it. It was still there, but it was horribly altered by the lipsticked scrawlings: FUCK SHIT PISS where my hair was, and STINKING FISH CUNT across my mouth. It had become a ravaged face. Raped by words. I would have preferred glass in the bed.

This was worse. There was the same yobbiness, the same pointless malice. But those kids didn't know me. They weren't my friends. People I'd bought birthday cards for. People who had shared the same bag of toffees when we went to see *Dracula*. I had been vampirised.

The next day was Saturday. In the afternoon, I walked round.
'He's gone to see *Reservoir Dogs*.'
'Again?'
'Yeah. He won't be long. Look, make some coffee. I want to get these reports out of the way. None of Grant's stuff is much good, by the way. We'll have to get her off our list.'

Chapter Seven of *First Person Singular* was on top of the fridge. He must have bundled it hurriedly there the night before. Gramsci strolled along the smooth uncluttered surfaces as I read.

> Maria climbed the dusty staircase of the old house. The bulb on the landing must have gone. She found her way to Ginerva's room by touch and smell, quietly pushing the door and breathing the familiar Chanel scent. She paused, whispered 'Ginerva' and then made her way to the bed. She could just see her in the light of the street lamps streaming through the thin curtains. She bent over and kissed her gently on the lips. Ginerva stirred, reached up and touched Maria's throat, sliding her fingers down...

And so on. As I turned the pages, some photographs spilled out. John had taken them a few weeks earlier at a party. He was always taking photographs. Jean and I were sitting laughing at a table. I wasn't shocked to find myself cast as a lesbian in someone's dirty movie. It's a bit surprising. But who wants to be used in masturbatory fantasies?

I let myself out. She could get her own coffee. But I caught up with him ten minutes later. I saw him bolt into the florist's. Had he seen me? When I walked in, he was paying for a large bunch of assorted dried flowers. They crackled as the assistant wrapped them. He looked warily at me.

'It's my birthday. I've bought a lobster.'

Had he taken the lobster to see *Reservoir Dogs*? I didn't ask.

'You're a fucking parasite, stealing my life when you haven't got the guts to write about your own.'

He took a step back, glanced at the woman behind the counter. She smiled.

'I need some Oasis too... about that much.'

'You're a coward to put in all those details about me and set your daft story in this town, so that people will recognise me, when you daren't even put your own name on the bottom of the page. Evelyn. Basil. Hilary. Beverley...'

He retreated before the rain of his pseudonyms. The florist was sawing green chunks of Oasis. I cornered him by the Arum lilies.

'And what about all that crappy soft porn?'

He retaliated, glaring.

'Writers do what they do. You must know that.'

'They don't rip off their friends.'

He picked up his package, his bouquet, his bag of lobster. Pink dust and tiny twigs fell from the flowers. He attempted a formal dignity. Flanked by lilies.

'It's clear that we understand each other less well than I thought.'

He stepped forward. Instinctively, I stepped back.

'Yes.'

My voice was getting scratchy. It wouldn't last out.

'I doubt if I could untangle your misconceptions. Maybe Jean could.'

The florist sniggered. He went on loudly.

'Obviously, I've let myself be swept away by the idea that we could exchange our work openly and freely.'

'Like friends, you mean.'

'You don't understand. Writers do what they do.'

I left. What was the point of staying? Anything I said would be stored in John's Apple Mac for future use. Future misuse and abuse. I didn't see him again, but I heard he was missing the Thursdays.

The phone rings. I answer, say my name. No one replies. Someone listens to me repeating 'Who's there?'. Then he puts the phone down. This happens three, four, five times an evening. A nuisance caller - nothing unusual. Just a pest. It's bound to be a 'he', isn't it? Now I just pick up the phone and listen to the man listening.

Tonight, when 'he' rang, I had a strange idea. Supposing - on an extension somewhere - there was a woman listening to me listening to the man?

ALISON SPRITZLER-ROSE

PENIS ENVY

Size doesn't matter
So I'll make this short:
One, please.

THE DEVIL'S SERMON

THE PRESENT political ice age is marked by catastrophes ranging from civil war to the minutest factionalism, from the racism which makes policy to that which makes firebombs in small industrial towns in the old East Germany. England, meanwhile, for Britain now is merely England, pursues an aggressive isolationism at the level of social policy while fervently inviting the economic colonialism which is a consequence of the distaste felt by contemporary Conservatives for the mere manufacture of usable products.

It does not require a very long inspection of Scotswood, Benwell, Consett or Ashington to grasp that in these places, where some of the unemployed, the never-yet-employed and the never-will-be employed of the old industrial North East live, history is certainly meant to be over. Here an entire class has allegedly outlived its usefulness. Coalmining, steelmaking, shipbuilding, heavy engineering - these are all extinct professions.

The recent refusal of the government to intervene (neither at breakfast, lunch or tea would it do so) and prevent the likely death of Swan Hunter shipbuilders - the last working yard on the Tyne and thus in the North East - was a refusal driven by an ideological viciousness which even at this late date is shocking (even for some Tories) to consider.

Tyneside, with only a single Tory parliamentary seat, is a lost cause for the government; and for that reason Swan Hunter, emblem of a tradition in extremis, a matter of pride in a region which built the world's navies - has been given every encouragement to die, no matter the contradiction involved when the consequences (i.e. the effects of a cause) of industrial decline and mass unemployment are savagely illustrated every night of the week in the streets of downtown and suburban England. It is not that the last eight hundred workers at the Swans yard will take to theft, violence and the latest poison; but some of their children might.

Classically, Conservatism is a political philosophy rooted in pessimism about human nature. Its libertarian individualism and its professed dislike of government are actually mirrored in action now by the increasing authoritarianism shown in anti-union legislation and the Criminal Justice Bill. The desire for control works in fact to produce the chaos it fears, and thus to fulfil Conservatism's hopeless prophecy - riots in London once again, the disconnection of the underclass from 'values' it cannot afford to espouse. As a method of disheartening and atomising 'community' it seems more effective than anything non-elected terrorists could come up with.

To talk now about social conditions involves a vocabulary that - aptly for the post-historical phase - seems close to exhaustion: cause, effect, symptom, responsibility, liberty, relative poverty... terms grown papery with use, mere language, which is neither wealth nor action - language unlikely to interest the housebreaker, the seller-on of bent gear, the twocker incinerated on the bypass or the girl selling herself round the back of the bus station. These people too are pessimists, and with reason. As they say in Liverpool, there's nothing down for them.

The language of consolation and encouragement offered by teachers, social workers, community organisations and the rest can come to seem as contemptibly empty as anything the government has to offer in the way of blame and condemnation. It is simply more noise to fill the purgatorial island where nothing is happening but the extension of the Law to emphasise the disorder which is its raison d'être. The Armstrongs and Charltons and Nixons and Elliots who live in the North East and have done since the Middle Ages are not unfamiliar with some of these conditions.

It was the state of economic ruin following generations of war which produced the feral, treacherous society of the sixteenth century Border Reivers, whose tribal criminality, a self-consuming cycle of theft, murder and revenge, brings many contemporary echoes. 'Bad news from the North' used to make uneasy the state which from Norman times had made the North a wasteland; it should be more than uneasy now, when the North, with its increasingly pragmatic underclass, is everywhere.

The Labour Party, meanwhile, caught in a dilemma which some of its leadership might privately care to consider tragic, chooses a formal rather than a moral solution. An NUM branch secretary in Ashington comments that New Labour disappoints him. He believes in a planned, redistributive economy. That is why he has been a member of the party all his working life.

But he is, we are told, a dinosaur. More to the point, we are told, he is of no importance. What matters is the middle-class voter from an imaginary Elsewhere, worried about the NHS - worried, we are told, for perfectly sound reasons of self-interest. So that's all right, then, as long as we know where we stand - where Late Late England means us to be, on the interior of a class system whose boundaries have been given a fresh coat of paint and a new strand of razor-wire by those who were meant to help dismantle them.

Cheers!

FIACHRA GIBBONS

SORRY FOR YOUR TROUBLES

I SHOT MY first soldier when I was five. I got him from the window of a cafe in Shipquay Street in Derry. 'Fiachra Anthony Francis Gibbons,' my mother howled. But it was too late. He was splayed against a pill-box holding his chest. He'd copped it point-blank from my battered sausage - *bang!* - and I'd eaten the evidence. Ireland saluted her boy hero.

Mammy was mortified, and gave the soldier one of the big smiles she saved for women in the street she didn't like. I wondered if I'd get a wallop.

Instead, she sent me out to him with my chips. I wouldn't have minded, but we only got them if we were good during the Saturday shop. Mammy said mothers who fed their weans out of the chip van were failing in their duty. It was only a small step to smoking, drinking and reading the English papers in front of them.

I gave the soldier my chips. He smiled and said 'cheers' in a great English accent like the ones in Coronation Street.

It was the picture of the wee fella kissing the squaddie on the day of the IRA ceasefire that brought the memory back. Once, photographers in a hurry paid children to throw stones. Now they want hugs, and we're very obliging. Always have been.

The next time my mother took us to that chipper was after one of the big bomb sales. They were terrible. You were dragged around all day as the mammies rummaged through tables heaped with clothes that smelt of smoke, while the men stood around smoking and getting in the way. All you could do was gurn while your arms were twisted into crimplene cat suits two sizes too small. Any cheek and you'd get a slap. 'You're not hitting that wean half hard enough missus,' the oul' wans used to say. 'I'd skin him if he was wan of mine.' Once, I got a class pair of socks with the heads of all the Osmonds up the side. This time, the chipper's windows were boarded up, but it was still open. The pill-box looked like a bomb had hit it, which it had.

By then the British had taken the high ground, barricading themselves inside concrete-and-corrugated-iron bases, and filling the local paper with pictures of chipped teeth, black eyes and unconvincing protestations of impartiality.

Boys in my class who came from the Bogside told stories of soldiers wrecking houses, as the Army raided and ransacked in search of arms which weren't there and an IRA which then existed only in the minds of a few bigots at Stormont and military intelligence, eager for an enemy.

Every night, I freed Derry in my dreams, accepting surrender from a stiff-upper-lipped colonel, who, nearly crying, would say: 'Jolly good show, Pat. We should never have been here in the first place. Kiss the colleens goodbye for me.' And I'd say: 'Don't worry Algernon, me old mucker. You shouldn't hold yourself responsible for the collective guilt of eight centuries of colonialism. Sure you can always come back on your holidays.'

There was an excitement back then, an innocence that ordinary people could right wrongs, that the overpowering case for civil rights would carry with no more than a few split heads. The News was great. I used to watch to see what shops had been blown up and if I could recognise anybody in the riots. My mucker Declan Breslin told me all about them. He had a boomerang.

But with every distant thump - a shoe shop spewing its summer range into the street - and every crack from a rusty, long-buried rifle, Frank Bough got more agitated on Nationwide. Paisley was going into raptures for civil war. As he called down the heavenly hosts, my mother prayed to the Virgin Mary for no unfair advantage to any side, especially to the Prods. Paisley drowned her out. The British created the Ulster Defence Regiment to back the Army up. The Protestants all joined. I remember my father saying: 'That will do a fat lot for peace. The buggers who were in the B-Specials and started it all get a government job and a gun.'

Internment. 'Armoured cars and tanks and guns/came to take away our sons/and every man will stand behind, the men behind the wire.' Me, Declan Breslin and Marty Doherty sang this when the school inspector asked us for the favourite song we'd learnt that year. We did detention for it. The master lifted Marty off the ground by his ears when the inspector left, kicked Declan and said I wasn't worth dirtying his boot on.

It was around this time that the concept of pick 'n' mix sweets made it to Derry. It was more like pick 'n' nick, because they only searched our schoolbags on the way *into* Woolworth's.

Conal O'Neill's father was hit by a rubber bullet. He had it mounted on the mantelpiece. We used to pass them around the class under the desks. They were great big things. 'See the bloodstains on that one.' 'Where?' 'Are you blind as well as dense, ye eejit?' 'Aye, I see it now.' Me and Declan Breslin sent one to Noel Edmonds on Swap Shop, but we didn't get anything back. The bastard kept it. Don't talk to me about the BBC.

It was all right at the beginning: we got the big gun reporters straight from Vietnam. But it wasn't long before their reports, which had plenty of mammies mouthing off and people in their kitchens trying to look normal - as if they usually peeled their spuds in their Sunday best - gave way to pale young English correspondents, standing out in the rain, telling us what they thought we thought - after a bit of prompting from Frank Bough.

I never missed the documentaries. There were loads of them about the 'badland bandit country' along the border where I lived. Investigative reporters would talk to men in dark rooms and discover that the grannies selling handknits by the roadside were using the money to buy bazookas for the Provos on Green Shield Stamps. Every pub was filled with bearded one-eyed men who sang rebel songs, and who - if you looked the wrong way at them - would have you shot. El Paso was nothing on us amigo.

My mother would never miss Panorama and the rest, they were great for home furnishings. A family would be interviewed - all squeezed on to a nice settee - in their front room, which you never normally got into except for special occasions like someone dying, for the wake. The cameras would pan helpfully from hands ('Isn't that a lovely engagement ring she's wearing!') to see if they had holy pictures or one of the queen, taking in the wallpaper, the fireplace and the cut of the curtains. As a mother would clutch a picture of her murdered son, Mammy would say: 'Wouldn't a frame like that be lovely for Fiachra's First Communion photo?'

Checkpoints. 'Turn off those effing headlights you stupid cunting Mick.' A soldier was banging on the bonnet and roaring in the window, his teeth snarling and white against his blacked-up face. He'd come from out of the dark, the ditch probably, his rifle covered in webbing. My father had been twiddling with his dip-switch; there was something wrong with it. We'd been stuck in a tailback up to a checkpoint for half an hour. A football match must have been on. Anyway they were determined to keep us all late for something. Daddy didn't say anything. Declan said his father would have levelled him.

My father had a crappy car. We went from a Cortina to a Marina. What a comedown. It was embarrassing being seen in it. To make it worse, Mammy put a Sacred Heart magnet on the dashboard. We all complained. It made it a Catholic car, it could get us killed. I stole it but kept it in cotton wool in a cheese box under my bed, just in case. Mammy never hoovered there.

Playing Spot-a-Prod out the back window of our Marina: 'He's not a Prod, he's not neat enough, and his eyes are not close enough together... Whoever saw a Prod with long hair and a pair of platforms... aye he is a Prod, look, he's going into Spiers' shop.'

Glenn Barr drove an orange Morris 1100 coupé with a black vinyl roof and sports wheels. Right nifty it was. He was one of the leaders of the Ulster Workers' Council strike that brought down the power-sharing executive. He was also big in the UDA. One day he came to visit his uncle who lived at the end of our road. I was having a kick-about next door and was sent down to the shop to buy him twenty John Player Blue - real Prod fags. He gave me two bob. Glenn Barr was great by me.

'Now smile at the soldiers, children.' We were going through the border post at Strabane, the Camel's Hump. There was a Scottish regiment on and they could be right awkward wankers. They really loved their work. 'They're only ordinary working-class people like ourselves, they don't want to be here no more than we want them to be,' said Mammy. 'They're only doing a job, probably the only one they could get, God love them. You've got to see it through their eyes.' But behind the steel and concrete, they were seeing you through the sights of their guns.

How to make a petrol bomb. Take an empty narrow-necked bottle, a milk bottle is best, and quarter fill with petrol or paraffin. Take a strip from a dry rag and dip in the remaining petrol, coating each side evenly. Stuff firmly into the mouth of the bottle, ensuring it is secure so none of the liquid leaks during delivery. Throw in one tangential motion, with a slight bend of the knee, keeping the arm extended at right angles to the body.

Paul McDaid showed us how to make them. He was from Creggan and deadly with a sling. We used to practise on sheep. His parents sent him to my uncle's farm in the summer to keep him out of trouble. He put wee bits of sponge and a squirt of Fairy Liquid into his petrol bombs. That way they stuck to their target and the bits of sponge burned into the skin.

Plastic bullets were harder and smaller than rubber ones, though they were still about six inches long. Not that we much cared. Only right dicks collected them. I once played soccer against a goalie who'd been hit in the head by one. Afterwards, he lets us feel the dent.

There must have been a safe house in the next street to us. You often saw young fellas on crutches or with their arms in slings going up and down to the shop looking bored. One day we were playing street cricket with the Moores and the Russells. They'd never seen the game before and stood watching as we batted a tennis ball about with a sawn-off hurley. They were from Armagh. We asked what were they doing in Donegal. They said they'd come for the weather.

A few boys' bigger brothers got caught up with the Provos. You never knew anything until they were caught. 'Who would ever have thought it?' my mother would say, whispering a prayer under her breath. 'Such a nice family. They'll be kicking the living daylights out of him tonight.'

I hated them nearly as much as the soldiers and the UDR. Between them they'd ballsed everything up. But when a guy I knew was recaptured after escaping from the Maze, I was sick to my stomach. We saw it all on TV. Mrs Coyle came running in from next door to say he had been got. 'His poor mother,' she said. He looked hard, but he wasn't. He was the only one of the older altar boys who hadn't ducked us in the bogs.

One night, there was a big bang out by Bonagee which left a crater in the middle of a field. Apparently they forgot where they'd buried the explosives and the rot set them off.

Me and Marty had gone into Quaver Records in Derry to get tickets for a U2 concert. It was the Sunday Bloody Sunday tour. White flags streaked with red paint, images of a surrender to peace. On the way out we were stopped at a checkpoint by the UDR. We gave our names. The soldier who stopped us was a big lug of a farmer. He started taking the piss. It was raining but he made us take our shoes off until he had 'checked us out'. Half an hour later another one came out and asked us our names again. Marty was spitting mad and said 'Patrick Pearse' (one of the leaders of the 1916 Rising). That was it. He had us down flat on our faces with his foot in the small of my back. Just as we were good and soaked he let us go.

When I was working for the local paper, an off-duty RUC man was shot at the bottom of the lane to his homeplace. He was stationed in Cookstown but came out to Donegal every weekend to help on his father's farm. He was a bachelor in his fifties and still a constable after thirty years in the force. He did the dog licences. It was pouring rain. He had been mixing cement and broken his shovel on the man who shot him. The gunman booted it back across the border into Tyrone in a Hiace van. An old man, his father, had laid a fertiliser bag over him and was scraping back some of the gravel so the blood could drain away into the ditch. He had great dignity. The Guard who was supposed to be preserving the scene was crying.

In the seven years since, men have gone on dying at a manageable rate in puddles by the side of the road or slumped on the carpet in front of their TVs. Now it's all over. What are we going to do with ourselves?

Gerry Adams coming out of a television studio in the States with a retired UDR man, the Unionist MP Ken Maginnis - the only one with the balls to have it out with him face to face. Adams tries to put his arm around him. Maginnis' shoulder stiffens into that stoop old men get from carrying too many coffins.

I can't remember the first ceasefire. I vaguely recall the footage.

EVA SALZMAN

A CLASS ACT

Four Weddings and A Funeral directed by Mike Newell, screenplay by Richard Curtis. Rank (1994)
Princess in Love by Anna Pasternak. Bloomsbury £14.99.
The Oxbridge Conspiracy by Walter Ellis. Michael Joseph £15.99.

> Six centuries of insect sex
> make hallowed rafters hollow wrecks
> - *Deathwatch danceathon* by Tony Harrison

WE WERE drinking at the Ram Inn in Firle, a scenic East Sussex village which is still largely controlled by Lord Gage, and his trustees. Apparently, this a concerned community, quick to spring into action at the slightest threat to its peace and unity - a failure to prune the roses or cut the lawn. Not as resistance, you understand, merely oversight. A meeting is called or taken - whatever the jargon is.

How telling that the local residents support and even welcome the opportunity to prove their loyalty to an aristocratic code which is, in fact, of their own making. So, the simple American thinks to herself, this is how the English aristocracy rules, by representing standards of legality and etiquette from which they themselves are actually exempt. In this way, the middle-class manages to reinforce its own status. I remember learning early, like most little girls, that I would never wear a crown. Though perhaps I never quite learned to know my place.

Meetings (an alarming and still evolving contemporary phenomenon) aggrandise simple dilemmas in order to obstruct their resolution. Meetings give illusory significance to the mundane. I think of the House of Commons' endless committees and sub-committees, answerable only to themselves, ideal distractions from the matter in hand: committees which allow themselves in camera privileges as if they were courts holding trials unsuitable for public viewing or involvment. I think of Parliament, its formalised procedural procrastinations, and the delight the members take in using these to their advantage. Of course, this is the American's crass and clichéd view of the English.

But this is exactly my brief, and this is only digression of a sort. The 'we' sitting around the table included a couple of writers along with staff from Charleston Farmhouse, the erstwhile Bloomsbury set's summer home, a place of little architectural interest apart from its fixtures and fittings decorated by Vanessa Bell and others in their spare time. Here I was, trying hard to look delighted at this latest conservation drive, this cause célèbre for the local history-mongers all dead keen to cling onto England's heritage: that shamelessly misappropriated catch-phrase, that advertising jingle, used as the grossest sort of palliative to the free-enterprise ethos of the Thatcher years. Meanwhile, real culture - ignored or overlooked - gets jerked along in the wake.

'Culture' must include the recent film *Four Weddings and a Funeral*, (a smash-hit in America) which introduced to the wider public a fine Auden lament. The script deftly drew a realistic picture of a group of old friends, all thirty-something Bohemians pondering the marriage question. But most of the English I know who enjoyed the film couldn't help commenting on its hilariously cosy English iconography, right down to the bumbling Priest, played by Rowan

Atkinson. Hugh Grant was perfectly cast as the charming hero, the perfect gentleman, the public schoolboy survivor (as opposed to casualty - how many of these have I met over the years) whose anarchy extends only to an inability to get to the church on time. It was all quaint and amusing; but let no American describe it as such. At the funeral, we got the one shot of the industrial North as a fitting backdrop for misery, before we continued on gaily to the happy ending. Personally, I like happy endings, but mistrust myself for it.

Optimism is a dangerous emotion. It is tempting to view any film renaissance in this culture as indicative of wider changes in policy and thinking. In fact, it may well be that the English film industry is only waking up since it has discovered that Ireland's Minister for Arts and Culture has been offering irresistible inducements to film-makers, in the form of tax incentives and location resources. The Americans have also cottoned on. Oh yeah - subsidy! I remember that.

Americans, of course, love 'quaint'; but they absolutely adore pomp and royalty. Sadly, we're not all Nancy Reagan. Surely no English person would regard the affairs of royalty as part of 'culture'. How confusing then that the yearning Mills and Boon yarn, *Princess in Love*, by Anna Pasternak, is published by Bloomsbury, a quality house. The book's purple-prose passion is set against a spectacular backdrop of hamfisted clichés - all true - about the upper classes: 'Apart from the full fleet of staff - the cook, the maids, the butler and the footmen, who paled into insignificance when they are not serving - James and Diana had the house to themselves.' Surely she jests.

Pasternak fawningly appropriates these clichés elsewhere, when she tells of Diana's first meeting with James' mother: 'In that marvellous stoical manner that only the British can muster, there had been no drama, no unseemly, prying questions. Shirley Hewitt had dealt with it as she dealt with everything, with tremendous aplomb. Her lip had not so much as quivered.' This is the height of disingenuousness, an affront to readers who have shelled out £14.99, and who would presumably show their humble origins in wishing openly that some decent dirt had been dished, some more salacious details supplied, for their money. I'd rather be unseemly than bored. Anyway, principles had better arise from something other than a ruling-class code.

Not that anyone expects such a book to be literature; though the burgeoning industry in royal kiss-and-tell books should tell us something about the changing times. Things ain't what they used to be. Or so people say. But they never were what they used to be of course. Princess Diana may yet be regarded as a people's heroine - albeit an unintentional one - if her amours contribute to fundamental changes in the role of the monarchy in this country. Not so far-fetched. Now Prince Charles has appealed to the Dimbleby dynasty to rescue his image. He has no choice but to go prime-time and into print in defence of his realm. The Royalty business is also one which has had to move with the times.

Americans are even more embarrassingly overawed by the sheer oldness of things. American wealth largely shored up the Charleston enterprise. I too have paid my entry fee to be shown around by a guide who was herself clearly awed by a house full of what are basically furniture-doodles, executed by a group of erratically talented artists, who, nevertheless, represent to many Americans the epitome of an elitist, eccentric, peculiarly English sort of Bohemia. All clichés contain certain elements of truth. But then again, is this not itself a cliché?

Take, for example, the woman who was my surrogate parent and friend for the two years I lived in Tunbridge Wells. She was a genuine casualty of the Bloomsbury life, the daughter of Roger Fry's last lover, and also the subject of one of Augustus John's failed seduction attempts, if not of one of his paintings. My parents certainly didn't know what to make of her at all, and I was puzzled by their response. 'She's… weird,' they explained. 'Yes!' I replied enthusiastically, 'Don't you think?' Her Oxford credentials only got half-written. She attended, but then found herself unable to leave her lodgings. She was presumably asked to leave in the end.

And so, a not-so-sharp turn through the college gates. I confess that *Jude the Obscure* was my favourite Hardy book. And for all the wrong reasons no doubt. The publication of Walter Ellis' *The Oxbridge Conspiracy*, has been the occasion for some splendid sniping across the bows. Mary Dejevsky, in *The Independent*, describes Ellis' book as 'one long whinge - the age-old cry of frustration from one who has not enjoyed the undoubted privileges of what outsiders call "Oxbridge"'. Tell us about it. Would she rather the poor outsider were robbed of a voice ?

She wonders whether the so-called conspiracy - which 'few would venture to challenge... given the preponderance of Oxford and Cambridge graduates in top jobs today' - is, in fact, 'malign or simply Britain's way of selecting its elite.' She ends the piece by suggesting that 'it might be that only an insider can tackle this question with any credibility.' Predictable, really. No doubt she hadn't intended to reinforce Ellis' theories, but there you go.

What is heritage then? It is scented soaps and pot-pourri, sterile exhibits of a past which is clearly the past. It is a harking back to a narrow value system. It legitimises witchhunts of the disenfranchised and marginalises what is actually a central group for these times - the so-called fringe of travellers and homeless - who are castigated for adopting too well the spirit of entrepreneurialism. Take, for example, London Underground's offensive signs which practically order the public not to give to beggars. We'd do better to include, rather than disown, this fringe, in our cultural and economic forecasts. The present so quickly becomes the past.

Perhaps people get desperate to hold onto what they know they have already lost - unwilling to accept the unpalatable truth that no one is in control when it comes to shaping history. English culture is in the midst of redefining itself, and no one may have the privilege of steering the punt. Though us artless Americans will keep trying.

STEPHEN PLAICE

SOMETHING BLUE

The Criminal Justice and Public Order Bill July 1994
HMSO. £17.60

I T IS significant that since Margaret Thatcher was elected Prime Minister in 1979 there have been no less than six Criminal Justice and Public Order Acts for England and Wales alone. This reflects how actively the Tories have sought to obtain public support through the manipulation of Law and Order during their fifteen years in office. It is a proven vote-winner. But what has all this tinkering actually achieved? Very little in terms of crime prevention, very little in terms of public safety. It has been the worst period of police history since constabularisation. We have seen the most serious disturbances in British prisons since the Dartmoor mutiny in 1932. So one might be tempted to ask (while one is still at liberty to do so) what might our society have been like without these refinements? More lawless, less secure? It is hardly conceivable.

Consider the main targets the present government feels impelled to legislate against with this Bill:

1) Child offenders of twelve years and upwards

2) Silent defendants
3) Ravers, Travellers, Hunt Saboteurs and Squatters

And then consider the main beneficiaries of this legislation:

1) Managers of contracted out prisons and young offender institutions
2) Private security firms

If we place these two groups, targets and beneficiaries, side by side, it is not hard to guess the government's intentions. Of course it is unconcerned that the prison population is rising again. Of course Michael Howard is quite happy to send people to jail for longer, to send twelve-year-olds to 'secure training centres', and to raise fines for drug-users beyond the threshold of the payable. Because it's good for business. For the first time since John Howard's (no relation) reforms in the reign of George III, jailers are now legitimately allowed to make money out of their charges.

How so? Under the 'contracting out' system the private firms that run prisons are allowed to cream off profit from the taxpayers' money that is set aside by the government for the management of prison and court services. In reality the new managers will cut these services and fudge their monitoring statistics to please the contractor, that is - the government. And as recent revelations from Doncaster have highlighted, the private sector does not necessarily bring in these services to the public more cheaply. The government will always help out if a private prison gets into difficulty and comes in over budget. It is inconceivable it would let privately run prisons go bankrupt while they are demonstrating their superiority over 'wasteful' state-run institutions.

Like any other business, prisons need customers. And what better way of drumming up custom than by criminalising those young people on the margins of society who refuse to work in demeaning jobs, to sit in overcrowded classrooms with poorly-paid teachers, or pay rent to extortionate landlords? Let's raise the fine for possessing their major drug, cannabis, from £500 to £2500. Let's ban their outdoor raves and have the power to arrest them even on suspicion of being on their way to an unlicensed party. Let's make it impossible for them to squat in buildings, including many council-owned buildings, that stand empty for years waiting for the property market to improve. If they won't conform and be conscripted into the New Standing Army i.e. the massively expanded further education system (now also contracted out of local authorities of course), if private profit cannot be made out of them at school, then send them to prison, where it can.

In fact it is more profitable to send them to prison. In Britain it costs more money to imprison a person than it does to send him or her to university. Thus, it is more lucrative to criminalise young people than it is to educate them. There are huge fortunes to be made for British and American companies out of those young souls by putting them into the new prisons just coming on stream. And just in case those prove to be too overcrowded, the government now has the power to turn your hospital or your school or even your house into a prison under the new act:

> 112.-(1) The Secretary of State may declare to be a prison -
>
> > (a) any building or part of a building built or adapted for the purpose;   and
> >
> > (b) any floating structure or part of such a structure constructed or adapted for the purpose

This clause must at least give heart to the depleted workforce at Swan Hunter who might now expect juicy contracts for refits of redundant British Navy hulks. Before long Mr Howard will be promising one man to a cabin and in-berth sanitation. If he does, let's hope he keeps it better than Mr Baker who once promised an end to slopping out by the year 1996. Still, on a floating structure, you can always slop out over the side.

What is so shocking about this bill is the breadth of its portfolio. By addressing a whole raft of issues, it is able to smuggle in isolated prejudices without the general public even noticing specific rights disappearing. How many people will shell out the money to read the actual bill, even if they can find it in their local HMSO outlet? (I couldn't find it in mine.) The English will simply swallow it. The only time they mobilise is when they are being directly taxed. And by targetting vulnerable sections of the population on the margin, the very *Lumpen* four terms of Conservative Government have deliberately created, Mr Howard prepares to roast his scapegoat till it stinks in the nostrils of his right-wing supporters. His bill will make little difference to the lives of the people it is designed to impress - the older and more moneyed generations. They will approve and vote with their boots on. The disenfranchised young and homeless will not. Such is democracy. Of course we have one. You can watch it freely debated in *The Moral Maze* in the comfort of your own home. Just don't try and debate it yourself, in the streets or on a picket line, without asking your local Chief Constable.

What side-effects will this tranquillising bill actually have on the somnolent subjects of Britannia? None, Mr Howard assures us. Our human rights are not infringed, in fact they are extended. We will all be able to enjoy our fields and paddocks in peace. We can eject interlopers who try to sleep under our roofs or under our stars. We will all have the right to sleep more soundly now that there will be no amplified music played at night at gatherings of more than a hundred people in the open air. And music, by the way, 'includes sounds wholly or predominantly characterised by the emission of a succession of repetitive beats'. And there was me thinking that was what music is. You live and learn with the Criminal Justice Bill, that's for sure. No loophole there, ravers. It's enough to make you squat. Or sab. But you can't do that now either with the new offence of aggravated trespass:

> 68. - (1) A person commits the offence of aggravated trespass if he trespasses on land in the open air and, in relation to any lawful activity which persons are engaging in or are about to engage in on that or adjoining land in the open air, does there anything which is intended by him to have the effect...of intimidating those persons or any of them so as to deter them or any of them from engaging in that activity...

Unfortunately this new right to protection from intimidation does not extend to foxes. Or gipsies.

Powers are also extended for the control of 'trespassory assemblies'. The most ominous subclause (70) increases police power of veto over assemblies:

> where the land, or a building or monument on it, is of historical, architectural, archaeological or scientific importance

This includes temples on land to which the public has only 'limited right of access', i.e. footpaths and bridlepaths. Effectively it is a ban on assembly at natural places of worship for those who wish to practise the Pagan or any other nature religion. How timely, when a new and redundant generation has just begun to wonder what lies beneath the self-denial and hard work ethics the Church has successfully propagandised in this country for the last fourteen hundred years. Is the New Age truly so dangerous that it must not be allowed to assemble at festivals and ceremonies, unless they conform to the strictest standards of security and have an entertainment licence? And what happens on Mayday, if there are more than ten people assembled around the maypole? Mr Howard is closing the open air. He is shutting the idea of 'outside'. There has been nothing as punitive as this on the statute books since the Game Laws.

What comes to mind is Forster's short story *The Machine Stops*. Our lawgivers are nurturing a population so domesticated and centrally controlled that it can no longer essay the world outside. Open spaces become threatening and lawless, a kind of medieval Wales. There be dragons. Certainly the Thatcher years did much, from *Crimewatch* to Neighbourhood Watch, to foster the impression that 'outside' is dangerous, as dangerous as 'the enemy within'. The Bulger case crystallised this fear for the following generation of young parents. Public places are no longer safe, because we are being encouraged not to think of them either as a) public or b) safe. Only spaces and venues in private hands, with licences, we are led to believe, have the level of security our children require. They are not even safe in a muzak-soothed shopping-mall. The streets are full of young criminals and beggars, the parks bristling with rape and lycanthropy. Best stay at home and watch television, where these very ideas are promoted.

One only has to look at the streets of provincial towns after dark for the proof. The streets no longer belong to the people, the fairs and festivals no longer belong to the people, not even sport is theirs. They are in the hands of the marshalls. There must be organisation, and an orderly return to your room after closing time. The people are no longer to be trusted with popular events. Like everything else, they must be managed and accountable - thereby removing them from the people and placing them in the hands of the powerful. The Criminal Justice and Public Order Bill in hand is the reinforcement of this insidious policy. And all this from a government that has put more people out into the open air than any other regime since George III.

Slowly, but no longer imperceptibly, the right to wander and to travel freely in this country is being withdrawn. Unless you are a car owner and a hotel sleeper, it is no longer your land to rest, sleep or worship on, even if that is still designated common land. These privileges will be reserved only for the rich and for those who conform to their culture. The gipsies (the Downing Street branch of the Ball family allegedly among them) have been gradually sedentarised since the compound system was introduced in 1926. Their culture has been systematically destroyed. The last thing this government wants now is a new generation of gipsies - a diaspora of young people the length and breadth of the kingdom in search of themselves and the ancient magic of their country. It wants them cramped behind desks or banged up behind bars until they are safely tied into lowly jobs, alcohol, marriage and family, and too tired to rave.

In times of Depression it is always the weak and the vulnerable that bear the brunt of the Reaction. One only has to look at the public fury that accompanied the Bulger case to see how desperately knees want to jerk in bad times. This time the young, including the very young, are also being singled out. Before they have even started in the world, they are branded as lazy, criminal and delinquent. The government is only too happy to legislate against them as if they were the cause of vandalism rather than the result of it. The police arrest them because they are easy to arrest. The Welfare State has become the Farewell State. If you don't fare well no one is going to help you. They'll just wave you off to prison.

The bill should gratify the thwarted disciplinarians in our society who call for a return to 'moral values'. It's OK to smack the kids. It's right to hate travellers. The dancing must stop before midnight. This kill-joy philosophy will please a nation of pleasure-haters. It will please the Nicelys sleeping soundly in Middle England, almost as much as it will please their masters in Whitehall. Though it is spread across many fronts, it is a direct attack on youth and on the hedonistic, drug-orientated life-style the Establishment fears young people will increasingly adopt as the Depression elongates and slips over into the new Millennium. What a sad piece of legislation to welcome that event. The next full eclipse of the sun is scheduled for August 1999. But if you go outdoors to watch it, don't stand too close to other people, or near old stones, and above all, don't make a noise when you howl.

PETER ARMSTRONG

A POSTCARD OF THE MARKET-PLACE

It's as sad as Larkin, mother;
the sandstone-fronted inns
are missing their commercial travellers
like family, the upstairs windows
yellow with the memory of nicotine.
Put an eye to the keyhole of the empty bedrooms;
there will be conspiracies of tweeds
and hip-flasks, parties closing ranks,
the decades hung in a lush monochrome
from Ealing to this sunlit dust.

Now the muse of Betjeman could go
in nice regret through dining-rooms
the Brabazon could lose itself across,
and big-thighed gels
stranded northbound overnight
might pleasure the glorious eleventh
and leave their skirts to rumple
in the fluff beneath the bed.
The Glasgow train thumps through singing DEO

and the branch-line rusts.
It's as sad as England, mother:
back to the absences and the grieving dusks;
back to the basic sorrow of the shires.

I wish you were here, or I wish I wasn't.
The breath is curling over my shoulder
in a grey scarf, and the Beeching afternoon
is chilling to a standstill. Somewhere
in these grey hills turning blue
the frost is assembling itself
in a repeated print of sleepers.

KEN SMITH

VISITING THE DEAD

THEY HAVE been dead for years, my parents, but all the same I'd neglected them. So it was time for a visit. I was overdue. Maybe I'd been a selfish and neglectful son, doing the usual things: getting and spending, bringing up the kids, taking the dog for a walk, exercising my rights and options, paying my contributions, every week buying my tickets to the lottery, wondering why I never won, knowing I was trapped, needing that weekly frisson of hope in sudden good fortune, its inevitable climax in disappointment, the forlorn hope carried forward to the next entry. One day Sam.

Oh they were alright, Mum and Dad, I felt for sure, but all the same I'd let things slide, and it was time, and I was overdue. Don't ask me how I got there, how I found them or where, or how any of this came about. Somewhere in England is all I'm at liberty to say. Just suspend a little disbelief, will you?

Fair to middling he said in response to my enquiry. Can't complain. I could, but who'd listen? He was leaning on a tree, resting by the roadside in the noonday shade, smoking a roll-up. Beside him crouched his dog, panting in the heat, an old black and white sheepdog. Nice day for nothing, he said, neither surprised nor disappointed to see me. They'd split up now, he told me first off. It didn't surprise me. They'd never got on, right to the end, when he'd gone out on a coronary artery occlusion, the result of severe atheroma, and the usual blaze of blind inarticulate bloody fury. He'd calmed down since then, I thought, and since getting away from her he'd felt more relaxed, he told me straight. Best move I ever made. Since then he'd wandered about, and hadn't done much: a spell as a deckchair attendant on the front, car park attendant, doorman, pizza delivery, the usual. Anything that left him with some sense of his own independence, where he could work on his own. He'd always worked, but now there wasn't much. He'd kept moving. He was still a solitary. He looked fit, weather-beaten, wiry, just as I remembered him. He'd always kept busy, couldn't stand idleness, in himself or in others. He was still the old northern Puritan, still the Victorian workaholic, the same tight stick with the same black Irish temper, the same shy unsociable awkwardness I inherited from him. And he was still a socialist, or so he defined himself, perhaps one of the very last, perhaps the last. Stubborn. He hadn't changed in all these years.

He hadn't lived long enough to get a pension, so he didn't miss that. As to the welfare state and the national health, he said it had worked alright in his day, but he was glad he didn't rely on it now. All those contributions, he grumbled. For years and for nowt. As for charity, he didn't want that either. He really didn't mind being dead, in more than twenty years he'd gotten used to it, and there was plenty to occupy him. He was content with the sunrise and the sunset, with the stars and birdsong and the blood-red roadside poppies in the wind, he said, a brief flash of lyricism. Such rare insights as to nature and history I remembered, though they had seemed more muted then. He'd changed and yet he hadn't changed. Just look, he said, spreading his hands to indicate the hills around us, the river below, the formations of the clouds passing over us, the endless blue heights of the sky.

And he'd gotten away from her. They'd finally quit, some years back, and not long after she'd followed him into the grave. That was the phrase he used, with a sharp glance from his blue eyes directly into my own, the slightest stress on the word 'followed'. I saw that, though he'd escaped her, he was still locked in their ancient decades-long marital battles, still nursing the old hurts, still chuntering to himself. That hadn't changed.

He'd just gone off, walked out we like to say, with something of a flourish. He left her to get on with her long games of Patience and her marathon jigsaw puzzles, Canaletto's Venice or Turner's Thames or some chocolate box Tyrolean landscape, her pots of tea and her knitting and crocheting and rug hooking, her gossip with the neighbours and her nattering and her Bingo. Though he was vague about the where and the what of himself, I soon realised he was homeless, sleeping rough, always on the move, proud and awkward as ever, and no he wouldn't come back with me.

Nothing to go back to, he said, for I had long ago spent what little he'd left behind. But he meant the world as he observed it now, an island of diminishing prospects and diminishing returns. He'd studied history: the history of theft, he called it. The great heroes were all bandits and pirates: the bloody Normans, Drake, Carnegie Mellon. They stole the monasteries and the monastery lands. Then they stole the common lands and ploughed the villages under and turned the villagers out as beggars, whipped, and the dogs set on them from one parish to the next, and then they stole their labour. And now look, he said, now they steal the water in the rivers and the oil from under the sea. They all belonged to us. We paid for them. They were ours. Now they steal the railways and the post office and the hospitals and the roads, and all they give us in return is this damned lottery and the dream of being rich. And he hawked and spat. A good one.

All changed now, he said, it was a place he wouldn't recognise any more, and he was content enough where he was. He began to gather sticks, and lit a small fire by the roadside. From his supermarket trolley of plastic bags containing all he possessed, he extracted a kettle, a couple of enamel mugs, a couple of tea bags and a tin spoon and a twist of sugar. Then, with water from a nearby stream, he proceeded to make tea for the two of us. He didn't need much, he said. If he fell sick he knew he must cure himself, for the state, so far as he was concerned had long since withered away. He shrugged. That's how it went. There were herbs about, usually good for something, and as he spoke he bent to pick a sprig of yarrow, shredding and stirring it into our tea. Good for everything, yarrow, he said. Good for everything. He'd learned much of this from the culinary and gardening sections of the Sunday newspapers he read, weeks old (for what use had he of news that was fresh?), and from sneaking into libraries - if only to warm up for a while until they chased him out - browsing on old herbals. He showed me a copy of Culpeper, and admitted he'd pinched it from a bookshop. His reasoning was he needed it more than they did.

He had a supply of aspirin, and various remedies he'd gathered from the hedgebacks. If he needed a tooth pulling he knew to tie a horse hair to it and the other end to a doorknob and slam the door shut. Either that or drive a red hot needle into it, at the gum line, and kill the nerve and with it the pain. He carried a bottle of horse liniment, for his aching bones, and some cough medicine he'd made up from docks and nettles, hips and hawberries, the curative properties of which - warding off sickness and stilling the panicky heart - he mentioned in passing. His old hernia problem kept coming back, what with being out in the open and all the walking. At night in the damp his old bones kept him awake.

But he seemed to have all he needed. He had a pair of my mother's old spectacles and a magnifying glass for anything he really wanted to study, which wasn't much. He was delighted not to be bothered any more by tax demands, rates, statements of account, any of the bills or their red reminders. He wore an army greatcoat and a porkpie hat, a steel watch and chain on his waistcoat, in his top pocket a thermometer and fountain pen (combined), an anorak and a set of stout tweeds over two sets of thermal longjohns, an assortment of sweaters and scarves and assorted gloves and socks, grey baggy underwear, a pair of Doc Martens, one brown and one black, and a good cudgel to defend himself with.

And he lived well, considering. He ate at soup kitchens or raided hen-houses for eggs and sometimes a chicken, scooped potatoes and other vegetables from the edges of fields, snared the occasional rabbit, a pheasant even. He tickled fish out of the river. There'd been occasions he'd been hungry enough to eat hedgehog, and once (he grimaced in distaste) a pussy cat. He slept in barns and hedgebacks, and in winter he sometimes stayed in a hostel in Battersea, but he'd heard it was closed now, (turned into town flats for young folks who worked in the City) and wasn't sure what to do in the coming winter. In summer he went down to the coast and slept on the beach. He was Mr Polly without the post office. This was what he wanted, what he'd dreamed about all his days. This surprised me, this secret old daydream. I'd never seen him as a romantic. To me he'd always been the hardhead, the butt end of realism, a practical man with no time for staring into space, imagining some other life than the one you had.

But it had all worked out to his satisfaction. He didn't want anything, not from me, not from anyone. All he needed was in the several plastic bags piled into the supermarket trolley he pushed slowly along, in no sort of hurry since there was no longer anywhere he had to get to in any sort of a hurry, his weight slumped forward on the trolley bar, rain and shine. There were a few other solitary wanderers along the roads he bumped into, from time to time. He could talk to them and exchange useful bits of information. Finishing his tea, he jetted the last mouthful onto the yarrow plant, put down his mug, and commenced rolling a cigarette using a paper torn from an old Bible and some herbal concoction he'd gathered in the hedges. He offered it to me, but I shook my head. He wanted to show me a few of his things, and rooted around in the shopping trolley amongst the plastic bags. He wanted to show me how he'd adapted, how he survived in nowhere nowhere land, he was still my father showing me how, and so far thank God he hadn't said either I told you so or One day my lad you'll wake up and you won't know what's hit you and I won't be there to help you. And he was pleased with himself, with good reason.

And he rummaged in the trolley and pulled out a builder's trowel encrusted in cement ('might want to build one day'), a spirit level ('for the lie of the land'), a steel spring tape measure ('got you taped, Sonny Boy'), a traffic cone ('slows the buggers down, that does, that will, sodding traffic, cars, can't stand the buggers'), a sign saying NEXT CUSTOMER, a box of computer floppies he didn't understand the use of and was considering ditching (and were they any use to me?), one of those pocket calculators that translates simple phrases between English, German, French and Italian (broken, he was 'working on it'), a set of old brass weights for a grocer's scale ('that's brass that, worth a bob or two'), a wooden crutch ('might need that one day'), a folding canvas stool, an army groundsheet, a child's potty with a peeling Donald Duck sticker on it ('belongs to a bloke I know in Brighton'), a box of service manuals for various washing machines and vacuum cleaners ('might set up a repair business, door to door, sharpening scissors, that sort of thing'), calendars for all the years he'd been dead ('records'), old war time identity card and ration book ('papers'), blackened stumps of candles, assorted playing cards, buttons, string, a pair of patent leather ballroom shoes ('you never know, you just never know'), woolly hats for cold nights (Tottenham Hotspur, West Ham, Yogi Bear), a torch ('battery works but the bulb's gone'), a tyre lever, a Swiss Army knife, an old car battery he thought he could get something for tomorrow, just down the road, across the brow of the hill, beyond the turn there, the other side of the river.

If he won the lottery, he said, it wouldn't make a scrap of difference to his way of life. So he never bought the tickets. Bugger their lottery. I don't think anybody wins. It's just another of the government's fiddles. All they want is your money and your marbles. And with that he seemed exhausted and weary of my company, and lay down and curled up in his greatcoat beside the dying fire, pulling the anorak hood down over his face, and turned away from me.

I went to hear her side of things. Glad to see the back of him, she told me. Always under my feet. She sat comfortably in a big old leather armchair, her feet in pink slippers with white pompoms. Good luck to him I say, if he thinks he can find a better billet. Before her was a jigsaw, beside her on a little table a pot of brewed tea, several cups and a container of saccharin and several boxes of pills and bottles of patent medicine, and by her chair various skeins of knitting wool she'd ask me, soon enough, to help her wind into balls. Your father, she called him. Miserable old bugger. She'd lost something, and kept looking down the side of her cushions for it, but wouldn't say what it was. She was fidgetting. Only happy when he's miserable. No bloody pleasing the old sod. Now she could get up when she liked and go to bed when she liked, go out or stay in, do whatever she wanted. And she slotted another piece into Brueghel's schoolyard, and she burped, one of those gut rollers she used to bring forth, much to his displeasure, one of the ways she'd learned to get after him, just to get up his nose, he being a bit prudish in matters of the body and its functions. Or so she claimed. She burped again. Baked beans, she said. And then she recited her usual chorus of Beg pardon Mrs Arden, you've got pigs in your garden, and Where 'ere you be let your wind go free, and Better out than in, Vera Lynn.

I found her cheerful enough, older, crotchetier, stiffer in the joints, resigned to her lot, brave with it, cheerful even. Thrifty as ever, she had stuff packed everywhere, in drawers and boxes and old biscuit tins: bits of string, elastic bands, hair pins, safety pins, straight pins, needles, hat pins, hair grips, metal hair rollers, needles, curtain hooks and rings, hooks and eyes, buttons, beads, a needle threader, thermometers, old keys, a matchbook like a set of gummed sticks for stopping a run in a stocking, hair nets, a few nails, screws, washers, plugs, fuse wire, worn out batteries. Stuff. Things she'd never brought herself to throw away. Things you can't get now, she said. Things you won't get again. She liked her things.

She'd put a bit of weight on. Her white hair was just a faint shade of blue. She was living in a big and very ugly house, in the worst taste, clad halfway up the outside with plastic imitation stone slabs, and the upper half pink-painted brickwork and the mortar bright white between, the windows criss-crossed by strips of black tape, and inside all brass lamps and purple flock wallpaper and everywhere her home-made rugs and waste bin covers made of felt and imitation fur she called Mr Dusty Bins. It was a messy house, full of massy dark brown furniture, doors and drawers that wouldn't close properly, and here and there patches of damp, crammed in with other messy houses in a bleak rammed-together section of some town, all empty warehouses and silent factories and boarded shops and drifting papers and little clusters of streets dropped here and there. We used to get Meals-on-Wheels, she grumbled. They used to send somebody in every week to help me bath myself and clip my toenails. I don't know what happened to the home help. And whatever became of Dial-a-Ride? It was any town with its Safeway and Iceland just across the motorway, through the scary echoing subway and up the long steps at the other side, the local post office closed down, the local hospital a great grey Victorian hulk with boarded windows and padlocked doors. You know the sort of place.

Forthright as ever, she hoped I didn't want to stay, as she had only the two rooms in use in this great house, no spare bed and no spare linen, and she'd nothing in, hadn't gotten to the shops all week, and if only I'd let her know I was coming. I'd have baked a cake, she said, grinning in the old way I remembered. I made a fresh pot of tea, and we sat by the two-bar electric fire, reminiscing, the TV pumping out the soaps and the ads. That's how they make them now, she said: it, the tele, so you can't turn it off. She told me that, if she won the lottery ('when' she won the lottery), she'd get a better place, bigger, with a garden, and a shed, maybe by the sea. And she'd have a dog, a little terrier. And go on a cruise, to Madeira and Lanzarotti. This wasn't her choice, this place, she said, waving at the walls. The stairs were vertical, I observed. Of course she couldn't climb them, she said, with her arthritis, and hadn't been up there for years. No idea what's up there. She'd let the top floor out to something called Unicorn Estates, which she said was the National Front. But they're nice lads, she said, and did odd jobs for her and kept an eye on the place. Only the paint they sprayed on everything in the neighbourhood brought on her asthma. And at nights they were sometimes very noisy, with their boots stamping up and down, and drumming. And the screaming got her down.

Time to go. It was already late in the afternoon, and she'd be wanting her nap. She was wheezing a little, but she had given up smoking. The day he left, she said, I smoked my last. I'd always suspected she only did it to annoy him. A fleeting visit, and we had nothing much to say to each other, as ever. Time to head for home. If I saw him again, the old man, I was to say hello from her, but not to let him know where she was. At the door, leaning down to kiss her, I realised how small she'd grown. She was shrinking. She was vanishing in my hands.

SEAN O'BRIEN

ON THE ROAD AGAIN

Dan Leno and the Limehouse Golem by Peter Ackroyd.
Sinclair-Stevenson, £14.99.

LONDON IS not the only setting for Peter Ackroyd's novels: there are also excursions into the countryside, but the city, 'brooding, secret, invulnerable', the distillation of death and triumph, indigence and vision, is the true subject of his work. *The Great Fire of London, Hawksmoor, Chatterton, The House of Dr Dee* and now *Dan Leno and the Limehouse Golem*: the streets and alleys, the otherwise unnoticed buildings found through peculiar archways, the maps that overlay maps, the vanished rivers, the hidden libraries and the blue plaque on the wall of new office premises - these are what really compel the author's passion. In comparison his human subjects can seem inadequate to their surroundings.

In a sense, of course, the characters are authorial pretexts for inhabiting the city, but their formal limitations also tell us something about the nature of Ackroyd's imagination. They suggest that Ackroyd is by temperament a poet rather than a novelist - a poet of the city, as Eliot or Baudelaire was, but at the same time driven and confined by an intensely English sense of literature and history. Ackroyd seems always to feel belated. It is not so much that he wants to be Back Then as that for him the here and now cannot be more than a rewriting, a reflection, a version seeking its original. His pastiches of historical voices and attitudes are at once expertly knowing, sincere and (at times) inert; he ends up in the odd position of being a nineteenth century postmodernist - a literary professional with the industrial capacity of a Victorian and the formal vocabulary of a contemporary critic.

These factors are both in play in *Dan Leno and the Limehouse Golem*, which imagines London as it was lived in by Dan Leno, the greatest of the music hall entertainers, by Karl Marx (who is interviewed by the police in connection with the Golem murders) and by George Gissing, the author of *New Grub Street* and *Demos*. In and out of Ackroyd's immese crowd scene flits the murderer - like someone from an 18 Certificate Muriel Spark - while in a storeroom in the East End stands Charles Babbage's great calculating engine, forerunner of the computer.

For Ackroyd, who is in a sense the supreme anachronist, this device looms as a symbol of knowledge, and of the inadequacy of numerical facts, but above all of symbolism itself - a cast-iron counterpart to Borges' Library of Babel. The urge towards vision which is always present in Ackroyd's work - 'such a vision of the street/As the street itself hardly understands,' as Eliot wrote - is found especially in the characters of Gissing. Walking the streets at night among the poor and the prostitutes, he feels that

> ... if the air indeed were one vast library, one great vessel in which all the noises of the city were preserved, then nothing need be lost. Not one voice, or laugh, or threat, or song or footfall but it reverberated through eternity... perhaps there was... a place where perpetual, infinite, London would one day be found. But then perhaps he has found it already - perhaps it was in him, and in each of the people he had encountered that night.

There are comparable moments elsewhere in Ackroyd's work: it seems to be what he is leading up to. The accompanying glimpses of the helpless poor (the eponymous founding inhabitant of Dickens's Tom-All-Alone's crops up in *Chatterton*, for example) sit oddly with the author's bluntly professed conservatism - oddly, that is, unless you consider where this intense, inclusive aestheticism might be leading - namely in the direction of Catholicism.

Rome is the aesthete's resort, where figure and ground, symbol and substance, and the claims of God and Mammon may be resolved for those who, as it were, lapse into belief. Such a lapse might prove to be one of the defining acts of the contemporary decadence so impressively, compellingly, but unsatisfyingly embodied in Peter Ackroyd's fiction.

U. A. FANTHORPE
THE SILENCE
(for Jane Grenville)

I suppose it was always there, the strangeness.
Once on a patterned floor there was a god
With ears like lobster claws.

And those vast savage roads, stabbing
Like swords into distance. You could see how they
Hated the landscape.

Still there, but other things are taking root;
And still at times, through stripes of sun and shadow,
The stiff dead legions striding back.

Some of it I liked. The big town arch, those
Tall confident letters, the docked words,
Imp. Tit. Caes. Div. Aug.,

And so forth. Nonsense now. And toppled, I daresay.
Nobody goes there. One thing I remember
Of all their words.

A slave told me the yarn: some man, on his way
From losing a kingdom to finding another, gave
A friendly queen his story,

And her people stopped talking, and listened. *Continuere omnes*,
Something like that. Stuck in my mind, somehow:
They all fell silent.

Nobody goes there now. Once it was full
Of tax-men, and gods, and experts
In this and that,

And the endless stone walls, sneering down,
Keeping out or keeping in? We'll never know.
And their magic unbudgeable mortar.

Strange beyond telling. They did so much,
Then turned their backs and left it. We, of course,
Can't keep it going,

No longer know their ways with central heating,
Water supply, and sewage,
And sickly babies.

They came too near the dark, for all their know-how.
Those curses they scratched widdershins on lead -
Asking for trouble.

We withdrew into the old places, that are easier
To believe in. Once we waited
For someone to come back,

But now it's clear they won't. Here we stand,
Between *Caes. Div. Aug.* and the next lot, expert only
At unspeakable things,

Stranded between history and history, vague in-between people.
What we know will not be handed on.
Continuere omnes.

Continuere omnes. (Aeneid II). Aeneas tells the story of the fall of Troy and his escape to Queen Dido and her court at Carthage. These words describe the response of his listeners. They were found scratched on a tile by excavators at Silchester, in North Hampshire.

THE DEVIL'S AUDIENCE

WITH U.A. FANTHORPE

IN ORDER not to strike terror into the local inhabitants, the Devil arrived at Wotton-under-Edge under cover of darkness, at midnight, and was pleased to discover that his lodgings were in Church Street. It was somewhat disconcerting to find a framed and illustrated poem by his interviewee hanging above the bed in the place where he usually inverts his crucifix.

After a restless night, punctuated by church bells telling the hours, and the full Cotswold breakfast, the Devil made the short step past the war memorial to the pastel pink house that U. A. Fanthorpe shares with her partner Rosie Bailey, who also acts as her editor and critic. The first half of the interview took place in the delightful garden, with views of the Edge. But, to confound the Devil, constant salvos of church bells were launched on the morning air by local parishioners. Cake was served. At any moment, it felt as if the Vicar might call and the Devil would be cast out for talking religion and politics at the table. But he plunged in. The first responses came from the collared doves.

DEVIL: What does England mean to you? Is it still a culture that you identify with?

FANTHORPE: Very much so. Partly because I spent about four years living in Wales, which I liked, but found radically different. And I began to see how England was also things that I hadn't noticed before, and I realised that despite everything that goes wrong - all the injustices - it is ineradicably home in a way that nowhere else could ever be.

DEVIL: Do you see that culture as being under threat?

FANTHORPE: Not in any way that hasn't happened before. My first training was in the history of the language, and that history has always been an embattled one. The Danes nearly overcame the English entirely in the eight to ninth centuries. There was the Norman Conquest - which knocked English out altogether for a couple of centuries, - and various other disasters, like the Black Death, all completely apocalyptic, in terms of the language. And yet English goes on. I don't think anything as bad has yet happened in our age.

DEVIL: But those cultural breaks contributed to the language. Don't you also see those invasions as positive influences on English?

FANTHORPE: Most certainly I do. It is one of the strengths of English that it can cope with all this, but it obviously can't have seemed so to the English at that time.

DEVIL: Do you think the new varieties of English that are emerging in our multi-cultural society will have a similar positive effect?

FANTHORPE: As far as the language is concerned, one of the things which struck me when I was in the North of England, in Lancashire for two years, was the way that the young Asians, in particular, spoke the vernacular in the way I would have liked to have done. They were really speaking Lancashire, and I was just speaking ordinary middle-class English in a boring kind of way.

DEVIL: Is there something underlying the culture that will never change?

FANTHORPE: Yes. The weather. There is a readiness to accept

what comes, which comes partly from a disposition that is encouraged by the weather. A flexibility.

DEVIL: You live in Gloucestershire in what the English Tourist Board calls the Heart of England. Do you feel there is a danger of two cultures emerging in this country? One which is rural, affluent and predominantly white, and the other which is urban, dispossessed and multi-racial. Do you think there will be an integration of these two cultures?

FANTHORPE: I think there will be an integration. I know it's on a bigger scale now, but, during the last war, there was a tremendous influx of Poles, and they were seen as outsiders - people we didn't want our children to marry, people called them Polacks - but now they're completely integrated. They do very well. There are a lot of them around here. On the whole, there is a great tendency to assimilate. Possibly there is a greater tendency to find differences between city dwellers and non-city dwellers. But it is important to recognise that a lot of the people in the country are extremely poor. They're not the sort of people who go to Henley and Badminton and that sort of thing. They have to scratch a very humble living, and depend on the DSS and their allotments.

DEVIL: How long have you lived here?

FANTHORPE: Twenty years.

DEVIL: How does this town fit into your general view of England?

FANTHORPE: It's a rather nice place to be. Because it's small. It's about five or six thousand people. Which means most people know each other. The essentially difficult thing about a city is that there are so many people you cannot possibly know, and this encourages a kind of fear. If you feel you know people, you are much less likely to be afraid of them.

BAILEY: This is a working bit of the Cotswolds. Not touristic.

DEVIL: How do you see yourself as a writer in relation to this community?

FANTHORPE: There is a great poet who lives just up the hill, Charles Tomlinson. People here haven't heard of him. They haven't really heard of me. If they have, it's because I was asked by the magazine *Country Living* to write an article about living in the provinces, which I did. And this has gone down big in Wotton, because I wrote about Wotton. But that's all. That's why it's rather nice to be a writer here, because people don't see me that way. I'm just the woman who lives in the pink house with Rosie and the dog.

DEVIL: So they don't see you as a spokesperson.

FANTHORPE: Heavens no. I'm not that sort of person anyway. I hope I'm a listening sort of person.

DEVIL: In your poem Neighbours, you say that you have to 'keep a certain distance'. Do you mean that? Or would you have liked to live in a Mediterranean culture, where people are constantly in and out of each other's houses?

FANTHORPE: No, I couldn't take the heat.

DEVIL: Back to the weather.

FANTHORPE: Yes, yes, I'm a Nordic person.

DEVIL: What was your background?

FANTHORPE: I was born and brought up in Bromley. Then the war broke out and we were all evacuated. I went to school in Surrey, which I loathed. The teaching wasn't very good, because at the time all the people who could get away went from teaching into the Services. We had rather indifferent teachers, so I more or less educated myself by reading. It was the sort of school where you were either expected to go to RADA, or something like that, or go into music. I wanted to go to university, so that was another struggle.

DEVIL: Was that struggle just against the school, or against your family as well?

FANTHORPE: No. My family were keen for me to go on. Because I was the only one who wanted to. My brother wanted to go to sea. No problem. But it was difficult for a woman to get in. They had a thing called 'a quota' at Oxford in those days. They would only have so many women. I particularly wanted to go to Oxford because it was the course I wanted: English Language and Literature. It was the language as well as the literature. In part of my course we had to work terribly hard on the OED, on derivations, where words come from, how they change - even place names - looking very hard, until you squint, at the individual word. I had never done it before. It's been the spine of my writing. I'm not necessarily going to use the words as they should be used, or anything like that. In fact, I find a great deal of pleasure and freedom in abusing words. But all the same, to know where they are, where they fit, is important.

DEVIL: You worked for some time in hospitals. Could you tell us about that?

FANTHORPE: At Oxford, I was involved in a road accident and knocked off my bike. I had to spend three months in hospital. That was the really formative bit of my life, I guess. Because there I was, in the orthopaedic ward, with people who were very brave, very funny. I think that's where I got the taste for hospitals. Much later, when I stopped teaching, I started working in the Health Service because I had to have a nine-to-five job and I thought I could combine it with writing novels. That was my idea at the time. I was a receptionist, the only receptionist, which is quite a solitary position. I used to think of myself as somebody in the trenches in the First World War, holding my head up over the parapet occasionally. Almost as soon as I started, I was overcome by the stoical bravery of the patients, and the way that the nurses and doctors saw everything in terms of being 'a professional'. 'Professional' is a word I have come to loathe. It is 'professional' not to be affected by people's misery or pain. There was absolutely nothing I could do for these people. All I could do was to try to find some sort of humane balance, to give them what they wanted - directions to the lavatory, where they could get some coffee, find a telephone - elementary things, like just listening to them, which weren't at all heroic on my part, but which began to matter more and more. After a bit, I began to write about the patients. I'd never been able to write poetry before. I suddenly saw that it wasn't important to write about me. I was put in the position where I could see other people - where, in fact, I was being asked to watch other people, it was my job - and that gave me the material to write about. I could tell you the names and addresses of all of them. I was simply writing about the patients because they were there. I became a witness of their pain and courage, and it seemed that if I didn't write about them, no one else would.

DEVIL: There is this sense that you wanted to list and record them. You have a kind of sympathy with St. Peter. Did you see that as a way of giving meaning to their lives, which the medical staff were taking away? You were humanising them while they were being dehumanised.

FANTHORPE: I have to be fair to the medical staff too. When someone dies, they want to forget, because it's a failure. Naturally you don't want to go around thinking about your failures all the time. I couldn't forget because in a way I'd seen more of the patients than they had, because they hung around in reception longer, and I'd seen them in a different way. That was another thing - language again - I began to take a deep dislike to medical language.

DEVIL: Did the hospital experience come to an end because you wanted to leave the institutional life?

FANTHORPE: I was there for eight years, and then the Arts Council gave me a writer's residency in Lancaster. I was there for two years, surrounded by healthy students. I couldn't believe they weren't going to drop down in epileptic fits. Then going back to the hospital suddenly became almost impossible. I staggered on for a bit - I'd grown inured to things, as you do - but I think the immunity ran out, and I suddenly found it as hard as I had done in the beginning. So I left. Going to Lancaster had deinstitutionalised me, and I couldn't cope with the institutionalisation again.

DEVIL: Do you keep abreast of developments in the Health Service now?

FANTHORPE: Not much. I got out five years ago. So I'm not up-to-date. I don't really understand it. It all seems too complicated. It was getting complicated then: the managers had already taken over. I didn't like the way they tapped our phonecalls. Counted the minutes we were on the phone. I think they thought we were making phonecalls to our lovers or something.

DEVIL: Speaking of phone-calls to lovers, can we ask your view of another British institution under threat. One of your poems is about the Windsors. The opening of that poem is 'Some people really believe in them', i.e. the Royal Family or the Archers. I understand that is an ironic stance. How do you feel now about the royal family? Does this country still require a monarchy?

FANTHORPE: I don't know if it requires lots of things that it has. I am historically attached to the monarchy. It goes back to King Alfred, who was just about the most brilliant ruler there has ever been anywhere. He saved England almost single-handed, not just militarily, but also culturally. I can't say that the present royal family particularly make me think of him.

DEVIL: You don't think that institution is in decline at the moment?

FANTHORPE: I think there's a lot of rubbish being talked about that. It's no more in decline than it was under Edward VII and George IV! I think to have somebody theoretically dispassionate is quite good, somebody who is really unconstrained by the forces of election. Power alarms me. I don't like to see people with power. But I don't see the royal family as having any power. And I think that's good. To have somebody spectacularly unpowered is how it should be.

DEVIL: You wouldn't see the monarchy as supporting an upper echelon of society, and giving it a justification for that upper echelon? You don't think it has discrete political power?

FANTHORPE: Honestly, I don't know enough about it to say. I don't move in those circles. I know it matters quite a lot to so-called 'ordinary people' that there should be this royal family who are, in a way, part of their family. There is a kind of personal relationship between people who never have any expectation of meeting royalty, but who nevertheless feel personally involved.

DEVIL: Isn't that something that's being lost now, because so many members of the royal family who have been held up as paragons of virtue are now being discredited?

FANTHORPE: That's just the press. People have more sense than to believe the press. I don't mean that they haven't done things, but I think that they always did.

DEVIL: Maybe it's the press that has created a belief in them in the first place. Or is it in the English soul?

FANTHORPE: The English habit.

DEVIL: Could you elaborate on why you feel that Alfred was such a great leader?

FANTHORPE: He was a great fighter, but that was just the beginning. He stopped the Danes, but instead of trying to get rid of them, which would have been impracticable - a heroic, silly thing that quite a lot of rulers would have done - he worked out, with the Danish leader, where they could be. I presume my ancestors were Danish - on the other side, as it were - but I think that Alfred was the great man here. He worked out the Dane Law for them - in Derby and Leicester and Nottingham, where they could be - without overflowing into the whole of England. As a result of the Danish incursions, towns like Durham were sacked, all the places where there were libraries, books, priests, any indications of culture. There was nothing left. He got monks from the Continent to start things going again, to bring Latin books. Then he himself started translating things into English, and interviewed sailors - a man called Ohthere - about where they'd been, so that he could get the shape of England, which, even then, they were a bit vague about. He was a great law-giver, a great identifier of things that needed doing. He put things right as far as he could. A man who could fight, and yet do all those things too, was very fine. He saved what was left of the literature, and gave it a fresh start. He more or less invented the shape of the English sentence.

WITH U. A. FANTHORPE

DEVIL: So would you say, then, Alfred rather than Arthur, made England?

FANTHORPE: Oh yes. I mean Arthur is just a myth, isn't he. I don't believe in Arthur. Do you?

DEVIL: I see him as an archetype in England. *Rex quondam rexque futurus*. The once and future king. The '60s generation, for example, would have said Arthur and not Alfred.

FANTHORPE: I think Alfred is more or less forgotten. Perhaps he will have his renaissance. I hope he will. Not only he, but his dynasty, though it fizzled out a little towards the end; he had wonderful heirs as well. I mean, for instance, Edgar the Peacemaker. His millecentenary was celebrated in Bath a few years ago. And Edward I, Alfred's son, was the man who united the whole kingdom.

DEVIL: Many would look back to the Roman invasion as the moment of unification and organisation of the British tribes. Do you see the Romans' occupation of Britain as an essentially benevolent period of English history?

FANTHORPE: It's hard to know, as such records as we have are nearly all military, religious or municipal, and in Latin, so we can't tell how the occupied Britons felt about it. The occupation was an immensely efficient operation, turning a Neolithic tribal society into a sophisticated one with excellent roads, coinage, markets, water supply, bringing a lot more land into cultivation, training for the work needed by a high culture - and underpinning it all, the tax system. But when the legions were recalled, the Britons, who'd lost their war-like self-sufficiency, were a sitting target for the next set of invaders, the Anglo-Saxons. It was meant to be benevolent. But there isn't true benevolence in raising people to a level of sophisticated living they can't sustain on their own.

DEVIL: So would you see the period of Alfred as the cradle of the culture?

FANTHORPE: Earlier really. I go back to old Bede. Of course it was all destroyed, but it wasn't really destroyed, because people in Ireland, people on the Continent, were keeping manuscripts, and they got them back again when Alfred came.

DEVIL: It's interesting that you see the development of the language as being synonymous with the development of the culture. There is no sense of the language with Arthur, for example.

FANTHORPE: Nobody would even know what language he spoke, would they. It might be debased Latin, or it might be Celtic.

DEVIL: Are you aware of New Age culture, which seems very focussed in the West of England? Do you have any sympathy with those ideas?

FANTHORPE: Yes, I'm always heartened to hear about people opening their minds in a different way. I'm depressed by computer studies and business management - people who only feel safe behind a keyboard - and all those dreary things. I suppose something of it is necessary. Rosie will tell me if it is. All the dreary things that seem to be necessary to keep life going. But I like to think that young people are making music, writing poetry, painting and doing it in different, exciting ways. I don't think enough stress is placed on this. There's always this feeling that what the young are doing is faintly lawless and undoubtedly to do with drugs. I think that the whole aspect of the creative imagination is forgotten. It's sad.

DEVIL: But the New Agers, particularly, would be very mistrustful of the literate tradition. They would see it as part of the established culture that they feel has squeezed them out. The kind of things that they find on the margin are much more to do with mythical, archetypal, more visual stimuli than literate ones.

FANTHORPE: That sounds fine to me.

BAILEY: It's merely a matter of fashion, isn't it?

DEVIL: But it has endured since the Sixties.

BAILEY: That's only thirty years, not long.

DEVIL: There are still waves of it. A lot of young people feel that literature of the past doesn't have anything to do with their present lives. They want very straightforward, colloquial - even harsh - language in literature to identify with. What value is there for them in the literature of the past?

FANTHORPE: It gives you a lot of different options. You can see other strategies and possibilities than the ones that are available now. Take the Anglo-Saxons, for example. They are so direct. They go straight for the thing. Life is absolutely bloody awful. They were interested in failures. People who had lost their homes, lost their place in society, lost their husbands or wives. Things always went wrong in the end in Anglo-Saxon literature. Even in *Beowulf*. He kills Grendel, the monster, in Part 1, but another monster, a dragon, kills him in Part II. You do not win. The best poem of the lot, I think, is *The Battle of Maldon*, which happened in Essex. The best speech in the poem is from a man on the losing side, when he sees the whole battle going against him. This is somehow inspiring to me. Because they went on trying, however hard things went against them. They didn't give in. If you give in, you became a *nithing*, a person of no account. And the worst sin of all in the whole book, for the Anglo-Saxons - who were only perilously Christian, they were more pagan than anything - was to commit suicide. Because that was failure. You'd given in.

DEVIL: In your poem about Christ, why do you associate the idea of Christianity with the demotic - the language of the common people - when it is usually associated with a more rhetorical language?

FANTHORPE: The reflection came to me quite out of the blue that Christianity was the only religion in which the founder hadn't written anything down at all. How odd that he hadn't. Instead of writing anything down, he'd chosen these totally unsuitable sort of chaps, who weren't capable of getting the message at all, who couldn't even remember the significance of a parable. And these were the ones that he chose. And I tried to take the thought a bit further: yes, I suppose that's why he chose them, because that's what he wanted. That was the kind of person he wanted.

DEVIL: Why would that be?

FANTHORPE: Not the literate. Not the powerful. Not many wise and not many foolish get into the kingdom of heaven. The unwise.

DEVIL: Do you think the changes coming into the Church of England are positive?

FANTHORPE: Well, I have to explain my position. I left the Church of England in the Seventies. Rosie is a proper Quaker. I'm an attender - someone who hasn't finally committed herself. We left, basically, because we couldn't bear the attitude to women. This was obviously before women priests. Also, the attitudes to war, to gay issues, the whole hierarchy of it all, all these things the poor old C of E is coming round to dealing with. But I wish they would stop doing it in such a fumbling way. There are so many encrusted individuals belonging to it.

BAILEY: It's a machinery.

DEVIL: Would you go back to it if it changed?

FANTHORPE: Oh no. I like the Quakers, it's where I feel at home.

DEVIL: How do you actually leave the Church of England?

FANTHORPE: Well, you don't. You just stop going.

DEVIL: I was wondering if there was a form I haven't signed.

FANTHORPE: Probably. That was under a particularly difficult vicar. We now have a much nicer vicar, who is a friend, which makes it quite peculiar.

DEVIL: Have attitudes to women and homosexuality changed in a town like this, and in England generally?

FANTHORPE: What one reads in the papers has changed, obviously, and in books. But I wouldn't say things have changed much here.

At this point, the church bells began to ring, as if to confirm the previous statement. Or perhaps to raise the alarm that the Cloven One was amongst them.

WITH U. A. FANTHORPE

FANTHORPE: The books in the library here haven't changed. It's only open three days a week. A place like Stroud is much more with it. Or even Nailsworth up the road. But in Wotton things don't change. If you mean are we accepted, yes, I think we are, but simply because we've been around for a long time. We're not in the rugger-playing, male-voice choir dominated region as we were in Wales, where we were immensely conscious of this unevenness.

DEVIL: The women's movement has gathered pace since the Second World War. Did you think there was a moment when it really started to have an effect in England, and on your own life?

FANTHORPE: Yes, things changed tremendously in my own life. I was immensely lucky. It was like being given a second chance in life, as far as I was concerned, with the women's movement. Because, although I had always wanted to write, I was rather daunted when I was at university by all the ex-service people who clearly had a lot to write about, and were writing about it. Here was I, fresh from school, ingenuous, not knowing anything really. Better keep my mouth shut and go away and learn! And I thought teaching would be a way of learning about people, which I wanted to do. The trouble with teaching is that it leads you gradually astray. You go in and think you're going to write. Gradually they give you more and more responsibility and power. In the end, in about 1968, I began to feel I'm going to waste all my life doing this and I know there are things going on in my head that I want to listen to. I'm tired of saying to people this is the way on and staying in the same place myself. I think it was the whole spirit of the '60s that was getting into me at this point, and I suddenly got the courage to drop out. This wasn't as brave as people are now kind enough to think it is. I could always drop in again at that point. There was always a place for a teacher. That was not just the women's movement, but the spirit of the times in general. The help to ease me out of where I was. And give me a second chance.

DEVIL: There is a sense from the women's voices that come through in your poems that they've been used to service. As in *The Poet's Companion*, it's usually the amenuensis, not the primary experiencer says to the woman at the end: 'You're in my way.' He seems to represent entrepreneurial man.

FANTHORPE: Yes, I do. I wrote it in the '70s, and there's a more recent one called *Reception in Bristol*, which is about successful businessmen, whom I find hard to like. But I'm well aware that the best poems take on people you don't like, and come to like them. I ought to do that, but I haven't got round to it yet. But I think they are the spoilers.

DEVIL: Is it not that we resent the modern incarnation of these people? I'm thinking of another poem of yours, *London Z to A*, about the roads into London through Lewisham. You seem to celebrate the drovers of Kent at the end of that poem. In their time, those people would have been thought of as the spoilers, as the thrusting entrepreneurs, the ones who'd bothered to get themselves out of Kent to sell their cattle. Might not people in a hundred years time be nostalgic about today's entrepreneurs?

FANTHORPE: I was actually writing about the pubs, but the drovers certainly would have come along that route. It was just the romantic name of the drovers which got me. I wanted to celebrate the changing endurance of Londoners and London.

DEVIL: Do we have something which we consider to be the English way of life? If so, the '80s seemed to be an enormous rupture in it, in the way that English people treated each other.

FANTHORPE: I really haven't the faintest. I was taken by surprise by the '80s, quite honestly. In the early part of the decade I was rather busy living, with the Arts Council residency, and taking in a different sort of people up there in Lancaster, a different sort of everything. It wasn't until I came home that I suddenly became aware of all these cheque cards and house prices. Being up there, I hadn't noticed that things had changed, and I suddenly came down here and realised that they had. I suppose that it began going wrong in the '70s, didn't it. One was conscious of a sort of openness of greed, which really hadn't been apparent before. I feel ill-equipped to answer this question.

WITH U. A. FANTHORPE

DEVIL: How important do you think it is for writers to write about social issues? Or do you think there is a wider role for artists?

FANTHORPE: People writing about social issues are really just writing propaganda. They're not really fooling anybody. Except perhaps themselves.

DEVIL: Don't you think you are writing about social issues yourself?

FANTHORPE: No. It never occurred to me that I was. You never really know what you're writing about. I don't. When I get to the end of the poem, I think: what the heck was it about? And sometimes Rosie tells me. I suppose all these issues are social issues. I write out of stupidity really. I don't understand things, I don't understand people. By the time I get to the end, with any luck, I might have got a bit further. But it's not understanding that really gets me going.

BAILEY *to Fanthorpe*: You're a very balancing sort of person. You don't go off in one direction or the other. You tend to see both sides, all sides, rather than going for the jugular.

DEVIL: So you think that art can never be polemical, because then it becomes propaganda.

FANTHORPE: I do feel that very strongly. I try to see not issues, but individuals.

DEVIL: Do you think that in your writing you have a peculiarly English voice?

FANTHORPE: I don't know. I have no perspective. I would like to have. I have been abroad very little. So I don't know about my language. My feeling about words is that I want to rescue them. This is how I felt in the hospital. I wanted to rescue them. They were being used as mechanical counters, but there were these beautiful things that I wanted to put in a place where they would actually work. I wanted to work them, in the way that a jeweller works jewels. So a word would spark off in different directions. I don't think I go in for very special words. I'm not a Jeanette Winterson, who has this fantastic command of the dictionary. Sometimes they're quite ordinary words.

DEVIL: How did you first get wind of the fact that you'd been nominated for the Oxford Chair of Poetry?

FANTHORPE: My publisher, Harry Chambers, rang up Rosie and said: 'Is it true that Ursula's dying of cancer?' So she said: 'No! She isn't. She hasn't got cancer at all!' So then he said: 'Somebody wants to nominate her for the Professorship. Would she like it?' So I said yes. Then there was a great gap, and nothing happened for an immense length of time. Then I began to get the odd telephone call from London papers and broadsheets, asking me to comment how I felt about it and who I would lecture on. Akhmatova of course! That put them off.

DEVIL: It would have been simpler just to say Blake. What were your expectations, coming up to the voting? Is there a process you go through leading up to it? Can you lobby for it, or issue statements to the press?

FANTHORPE: Oh yes. You can do all these things. But we didn't. Somebody did. He wrote to every single person on the register, and got rather a knock on the knuckles for it. Apparently there are certain ways of doing this, you see, gentlemanly ways.

BAILEY: It's one of these essentially amateur Oxford larks.

DEVIL: Did you think there was a realistic possibility that you might get it?

FANTHORPE: No, no. James Fenton had stood for it ten years before, and obviously was on hand - I mean he lives at Cumnor and he presumably knew all the people - and there would be a big Oxford vote for a local man and a man who writes for an important paper. So I didn't really think I'd get it. As I was the first woman to be nominated, ever, I thought it would be wrong not to have a bash. So I did. I hope it was good publicity for Peterloo. It was interesting to see the press at work. And I enjoyed being at James' party, because he's very rich, and there was a grand garden and marquee, and people like Lord Gowrie and Jonathan Miller and Salman Rushdie with his minders. This is not the sort of life we lead...

BAILEY: Not that we actually met them, you understand.

FANTHORPE: No, but we saw them. They were there. We were in the same place.

DEVIL: Would you have enjoyed it if you had been successful?

FANTHORPE: There's a little bit of the teacher left in me, enough to enjoy working with people who write, which I could have done, as Professor, as Auden did. The poets I would really like to read about, think about, talk about, are Basil Bunting, David Jones, Stevie Smith, Emily Dickinson...

BAILEY: People on the edges.

FANTHORPE: That's right. Cowper. Crabbe. William Barnes. Christopher Smart. People who tend to get left out of things. And Browning of course, because Browning is the big man for me.

DEVIL: Why would you choose people who have been left out?

FANTHORPE: Partly because they do get left out, and therefore have something to say that hasn't been properly heard. Those who are not seen as wanted on voyage, who have somehow not been fully assimilated into 'what you expect the young person to know'.

DEVIL: Do you think that being an outsider - or being mad or unhappy - is a prerequisite to creating artistic work?

FANTHORPE: No. I don't know what the prerequisites are. As a writer myself, I find the ones who didn't make a great success of it in their own lifetimes are the ones who strike me. I mean - not Tennyson. Probably not Eliot. Basil Bunting is a kind of poor man's Eliot. Most people haven't even heard of David Jones. The fact that they weren't officially successful might mean that they were extremely successful in other ways, which were not acknowledged.

BAILEY: It's a matter of luck entirely.

FANTHORPE: Hopkins just popped into my mind. He obviously

has a terrific success now, but he saw himself as a complete and utter failure.

DEVIL: Do you see yourself as an outsider?

FANTHORPE: Oh I think so, yes.

DEVIL: But if you had been appointed Poetry Professor, then you would have been an insider.

FANTHORPE: I should still have felt outside. They would have been university people - dons or MAs, dining at high table. That is totally foreign to our way of life. I have deep misgivings about what universities do to English studies anyhow, and I should feel very compromised if I belonged to that. I was going to say that the sort of people we meet when we are away from home are, on the whole, poets, and how kind and thoughtful and generous they are. This is another rather curious aspect of our lives, that they are such nice people. I always expected the literary world to be very cut-throat.

DEVIL: But you're outside of it.

FANTHORPE: True. And also, of course, there's no money in poetry, so there's no reason why anyone should be aggressive.

DEVIL: Sometimes the lesser the rewards, the sharper the knives.

FANTHORPE: If England treated its writers as Ireland treats its writers, or as Australia and America treat their writers, or even Scotland, we'd be on to a better wicket, wouldn't we?

DEVIL: Keats says in his letters that England pushes its writers into the byways. He describes them like violets in the hedgerows. It has this romantic tinge to it. In one sense it's a complaint, but in another sense, he's saying this is where they ought to be, in the margins.

BAILEY: A mixture of irrelevance and significance.

FANTHORPE: If you were a poet on the inside, you'd become Alfred Lord Tennyson.

DEVIL: You seem to have a very polemical line on Tennyson. In your poem about his death, when we're expecting the usual valediction of a great poet, instead, we get consideration of ordinary, insignificant deaths. Does he represent more than just himself, in your poem about his death?

FANTHORPE: He represents the poet who made it in society, doesn't he. He became a Lord. He published a great many books. Quality unspecified. And bought a big house. I like Browning better. Put it like that.

DEVIL: Going from the sublime to the ridiculous, do you try to incorporate balance into the structure of the poems themselves ? In the first part of the poem Patience Strong, you adopt an unusually aggressive stance, but then suddenly put some weights in the other pan, when you describe a patient who has taken sustenance from this very clichéd world that Patience Strong presented in her writing. Did you set out to achieve the balance, or did you get halfway through and think, no, I'm going to find something to rescue the usefulness of Patience Strong.

FANTHORPE: The Tennyson one I wrote bing, bang, bong, at the beginning. Have a go at Tennyson. And then halfway through I thought I couldn't, and had to change. The Patience Strong one, that was a real, true life story, as they say. Obviously what I really knew was the second part, the bit about the chap. But I had great difficulty writing the first part, because I couldn't see how I could lead into it, until it became clear to me that I had to have a bash at Patience.

DEVIL: But you have actually redeemed Patience Strong by the end.

FANTHORPE: Well, you know, that's what he said. And I had to respect what he said.

DEVIL: We see that notion of balance, and of looking at both sides of the argument, as quite an English attribute.

FANTHORPE: I'm terribly sorry. Although yes, I am English - I've lived pretty well every day of my life in England - it's not a sort of thing I am able to assess from the outside. Nobody has ever said to me: You're very English. You don't see if you're not in some sense or another outside, if you're firmly integrated inside society.

DEVIL: But ultimately, in the Patience Strong poem, don't you suppress any possible emotions or aggressions you might have had, giving the poem over to that other person?

FANTHORPE: I know I do this. I hand over to the other person. I think I learned it back at Oxford, from Chaucer and Wordsworth, who both tend to do that. So perhaps this is another English characteristic. Chaucer, for example, makes a fool of himself in *The House of Fame*. Flying on the eagle's back, he gets bested in argument by a mere bird. And he's the only one of the pilgrims in the *Canterbury Tales* who doesn't actually manage to get through his story. His story is so awful that they shout him down. And Wordsworth is always being proved wrong by small children and leech-gatherers. I've always found that moving. That the poet doesn't have the last word.

DEVIL: Is that a negation of self?

FANTHORPE: I don't think so. It feels as if I'm being honest. I wouldn't claim that it is honest, but I would like to be honest. It's something I work towards.

DEVIL: What do you think about confessional poetry?

FANTHORPE: I've never found it frightfully interesting. But I think it's important that it should be there. There are valuable things that people probably need to write about in the confessional mode. I've always tried to avoid it myself, because I felt that what I was wasn't really interesting in itself, that the people I saw were the interesting thing, and I was there yet again as a recorder.

DEVIL: Is there a portion of your work that you consider to be more confessional the rest? I'm thinking of the poem *Doubles*. It contains some disturbing inverted images of the eye.

FANTHORPE: I wrote it when I was depressed. There are a couple of others, *Descent* and *Sentences*. To be perfectly honest, I

WITH U. A. FANTHORPE

hardly remember how I wrote them. I certainly wouldn't be very well able to tell you what they mean, because I was on medication. You can probably account for them better than I can. 'The eye in its orbit walks upside down'. I believe it's scientifically true, isn't it, that we see things upside down and the brain transfers the news. In that poem, the traveller in the tunnel sees her shadow just the other side of this rather thick glass, and strange things are going to happen to the shadow as much as to her. I write through this dark tunnel of unknowing. That's the pleasure of it, finding out what's going to be there. If you know what's going to be there, there's no fun. You might just as well write it in prose. It's exploring. I would have liked to have been an explorer. Exploring into the darkness. That's what I really like.

DEVIL: There is a sense of loss, of a kind of collective culture, in your poem about Cecil Sharp, the collector of English folk songs. He was another recorder. You must see yourself, to some extent, in his tradition. You talk about a kingdom there. You mean presumably the kingdom of folklore and folk-song. You're not extending that any further, making it a cipher for the Empire, or the United Kingdom?

FANTHORPE: It never occurred to me at all, to be honest. Obviously there's nothing to stop people from reading that into it. What really interested me was the fact that a lot of the things that are lost hang around. That's why I mentioned the Roman villas in the first part of the poem. The folk-song had been such a demotic thing - it depended entirely on the people who sang it, it had never been written down -- and Cecil Sharp and Vaughan Williams were just in time to pick it up. I was interested in that balance really.

DEVIL: You seem to value the historical demotic, but not the contemporary demotic. In that poem you say that another generation comes along and puts the needle on the gramophone.

FANTHORPE: That was people not valuing what their parents and grandparents had automatically, in the way that younger generations don't. That was all I meant there. And those younger people were the young of the early years of this century, when folk-song seemed old-fashioned.

DEVIL: Isn't there a cycle? Generations don't recognise the past when they're young, but do again, as they grow older.

FANTHORPE: Probably there is. If people live long enough, they will come back to be respected. Not particularly in the case of folksong, alas. Quite a lot of writers go through this trough in their middle years, and then come back at the end, and are tremendously revered, just because they have grown to be old.

DEVIL: At the end of your poem about the death of folk-song, what actually drowns out the very strong tradition Sharp had unearthed - and which you had continued by writing a poem about Sharp - are the voices of the Women's Institute Choir at the Albert Hall.

FANTHORPE: And the folk-song industry. Industry is the crucial word there. Money. Yes.

DEVIL: But that choir, those voices of middle England, they might be some of your generation, your neighbours.

BAILEY: You've just eaten their cake.

DEVIL: At the end of *Earthed*, there are the lines 'This narrow island charged with echoes/and whispers snares me'. Is that your summing up of England?

FANTHORPE: It's my summing up of me. I'm hopelessly here. But it's not a statement about England itself. It's a statement of how I feel about England.

WITH U. A. FANTHORPE

The interview in the bag, the Devil walked out into the broad daylight. On the narrow pavement he was obliged to step aside to allow a wedding party to pass by on their way to the Church. They paid him no heed in their eagerness to attend the traditional ceremony. There was something appropriate in this image on the Devil's eye. He left Wotton-under-Edge and took the road for Gloucester, where he was later sighted asking directions to Cromwell Street.

EMILIA DI GIROLAMO

THE SPELL

Witchcraft in Buckinghamshire

IT IS difficult to recall a time when Selina was not a witch. I am sitting on the step by the back door as the sun dips behind a cloud that threatens rain over this Buckinghamshire council estate. All the houses are the same, grey concrete boxes with unkempt gardens and rusty cars abandoned in the driveways. Selina is walking widdershins around a large black cauldron which boils and bubbles, tapping the rim rhythmically with her athemy, prodding the large green flames now and then. She adds a handful of lizard's leg and a little eye of newt, muttering an incantation quietly under her breath.

My sister, Selina. Eighteen months my senior, though I often think of her as my younger sister. Italianate eyes, Roman nose, pale complexion framed by long centre-parted hair, tinged with henna. She is clad in her everyday wear - jeans, clogs, headscarf and ethnic print blouse in jade and red. She has an array of silver on her hands and a pentacle on her neck. My sister, High Priestess to the Goddess.

There is a sudden hiss from the cauldron as the flames, apparently unprovoked by any physical activity, leap up with a flash of blue, and one of the brass knobs on the outside of the cauldron flies off, missing me by an inch. I stop laughing. 'Oh I'm sorry, bloody thing, it keeps doing this, I'm going to have to get a new one. I've nearly finished anyway, I'll just put the cauldron out and then I'll put the kettle on. I can bury this later. I bought the most gorgeous dress, I might wear it for the Autumn Equinox, I must show you.'

I call out 'Hello!' to the little boy who has suddenly appeared in next door's garden. He is clutching a toy truck in one hand and making toy truck noises as he zooms around the garden. He stops and looks from me to Selina, then over to her familiar, the black cat Opium blinking silently in the herb garden. 'Hello', I say again. The little boy begins to back away towards his house, eyes huge with fear.

'MUMMY, MUMMY! There's a WITCH next door!'

I can hear his mother in the kitchen, laughing at his childish imagination. I laugh with her, remembering how scared I was of Selina when I was a child.

Even then I secretly envied my sister. It was Selina who chatted happily with our dead great grandmother, predicted relatives' deaths, foretold the future and healed childhood injuries. During the day I would happily play her accomplice, but at night I would shake with fear, cowering beneath the bed sheets, afraid some ghostly grey shape might appear..

Selina, who had no fear of the dark, had told me enthusiastically that a leyline ran through the corner of my room and that something was bound to manifest itself before long. She thought I would be thrilled but instead I lay with my eyes shut tight. Lucifer's laughing face would appear in my mind. Either way there was no escape, open or closed. I lay there, confessing my sins to a God I wasn't even sure existed but feared far more than any devil.

Forgive me Father for I have sinned. It's been twenty years since my last confession.

My father was a Catholic, but family tradition has it he was descended from the revolutionary priest Girolamo Savonarola who was burnt at the stake for his heretical beliefs. My father's father met the same fate when the Abbruzzese fireworks factory where he worked spontaneously combusted in the Thirties.

As a child Papa would pass the house of *La Strega*, the witch, and each day the smell of the carnations that adorned her garden became more inviting. Drunk on the aroma and persuaded by his friends, he dared to pick one of the forbidden blooms. The witch saw him and came out of the house. The other boys ran off and Papa, the seven-year-old child, stood in front of the wise woman of the village. She did not scold him but invited him into her house and told him a secret. She said she had chosen him to impart her powers to, and that if he wanted to be wise and strong he must swallow the heart of the *rondinella* (the swallow) while it was still beating. An appointment was arranged. The ritual was duly performed. My father ran from the house to vomit violently, sick at the cruelty and frightened by the witch's words.

But just as the witch had promised, he became strong and earned the nickname *Aquilla Nera*, the Black Eagle. He came from an artisan background, but after emigrating to England, the Black Eagle rose to become an outstanding athlete, footballer and boxer. Later, as a successful painter, he was knighted by the Italian government for his outstanding services in the fields of art and education. He now jokes about his 'powers' and dismisses such things as nonsense, but he has never lost his psychic ability to predict events.

On my eighteenth birthday he gave me a Fiat 127. So that Selina would not be envious he bought her a broomstick. Even though 'the powers' are traditionally thought to be passed matrilinearly, in our family this was not the case. The powers given to him by *La Strega* he handed down in turn to my sister. While I spent all the time with my mother, Selina was always *figlia di papá*, Daddy's girl.

Selina and I had our own club with passwords and membership cards. But, unlike the clubs our peers formed, ours was not influenced by Enid Blyton's *The Famous Five*, nor by *The Secret Seven*, but then these were not the books of our childhood. With a mother that read us John Wyndam's *The Day of the Triffids* as a bedtime story when we were six and seven respectively, what could one expect?

Our club was called the W W Club, the White Witches. Selina and I took great pride in its rituals. At school we would communicate telepathically, influenced by Wyndam's *Chocky*. At home we would invent magical lands borrowed from Narnia which we visited through the back of the wardrobe just off the leyline in my room. We sought out graveyards, intrigued by the presence of the dead; we revelled in local murder cases and supposedly haunted sites. Our childhood heroines were strong subversive women from the literature read to us by our mother: Hardy's Tess, Bronte's Jane Eyre and Austen's Lydia from *Price and Prejudice*.

Even our Italian Catholic grandmother did not force her religion upon us but told us colourful stories of Civitella, the village she came from, where witches and werewolves were commonplace Every village had a wise woman who would offer spiritual advice and perform spells to heal or rid the afflicted of *l'occhio male*, the Evil Eye.

Halloween was a particularly special time for us, a celebration, (our favourite time of year). Not for us trick-or-treating local neighbours and gaining bags of booty, or scaring friends with plastic masks and fake blood - no such commercial rubbish for us. Led by Selina, we would don black cloaks and pointed hats - lovingly cut from newspaper and painted by our mother - and clutch home-made broomsticks heading off into the wild, dark garden to dance around our parents' cauldron-shaped coal scuttle with our cats, Gobbolino and Carbonell (named after witches' cats from popular kids' fiction). As it got dark we would chant and sing to the moon.

Witchcraft is often falsely regarded as the antithesis of Christianity or as an alternative religion. In itself it is not a religion, but a vocation, in much the same way as the priesthood within Christianity. Witches occur within the religion of Paganism. The word 'pagan' in Christian culture is always used in a derogatory context, implying an absence of religion. This is blatant prejudice, the word actually means 'of the land' and is now used by pagans like Selina to describe an eclectic, nature-based, Goddess-centred religion. But its polytheism encompasses all religious beliefs, including Christianity.

If it is such a peaceful, inclusive religion, why is it so often presumed that Pagans, and Witches especially, are devil-worshippers? Pagans do not worship the 'devil' because the devil is a predominantly fictitious aspect of Christianity, which Pagans do not acknowledge. This common prejudice emerges from the fundamentalist Christian view that everything that exists without Christ must be satanic. In fact the masculine deity of the Pagans, sometimes symbolised by the Green Man, shares attributes with the Christian devil, such as Pan's horns and hooves. This is not surprising. Christian propagandists took the image of the Green Man and attached it to their Satan, depicting him as an evil serpent at times when it was politically and economically advantageous to turn people away from the Old Religion. The spiritual and symbolic resemblance between the Horned One and the Christ figure (a deity who is usually acknowledged by Pagans) is infinitely more apparent. Both were born amongst the beasts of the field, to a single woman, in a cave or other humble place. Both were crowned with vegetation and are synonymous with solar energy. Both were sacrificed on the tree of life and rose from the dead, leaving a legacy of healing and blood ritual as communion.

The image of witchcraft that exists in the popular imagination was reinforced by ecclesiastical propaganda during the 'Burning Times', predominantly in the fifteenth century when witches and women suspected of being witches were tried, invariably found guilty, then burnt or drowned. In the modern age these false images are still underscored by children's stories concocted to scare or amuse the new generation before they have time to find the religion themselves. In later life we meet these images again in the form of horror films and books which rely on public ignorance of the 'herstory' behind witchcraft to sell patriarchal titillation, fear and violence. I recall as a teenager seeing a Hammer House horror film where a witch was presented as a woman with an insatiable sexual appetite who scarred her lovers' backs with her long nails and ate raw liver dripping with blood.

Unfortunately the 'factual' information pertaining to the witch trials has come down to us from the accounts of the persecutors themselves. The raving paranoia recounted in the ecclesiastical records has led modern historians to dismiss the witch trials and indeed withcraft itself as neurotic 'hysteria' (this word is derived from the Latin for womb - *hystera*. It was coined by men to imply that the source of a woman's frenzy was her womb).

The church records are indeed horrific. Children were used as informers upon their mothers, often tortured until they would comply. Daughters and infants were executed with their mothers. But boys were made to denounce their mother, and in Europe and Scotland, to dance on the smouldering embers around her molten remains one hundred times. Burning and torture were not authorised by English law. Nevertheless the dispersal of a victim's family and possessions, the starvation of her children and the denial of food and water, must have been torture enough, not to mention the sexual abuse and gang rape which occurred quite openly to women held prisoner accused of witchcraft.

In the '90s such treatment is unlikely, but witches are still forced into secrecy. It is five hundred years since nine million of them were murdered, forty years since witchcraft was decriminalised and only five years since satanic abuse investigators refused to acknowledge the difference between witches and satanists. Witches are still persecuted by fundamentalists and extremists as well as by the media. So they cannot be as open about their religion as, say, a Roman Catholic can.

Nobody 'becomes' a witch. Witches *are*. People may recognise experiences which lead them to the conclusion that they belong within the craft. Witches believe they are reincarnated as witches and often retain memories of these past lives. Paganism is a passive religion, in the sense that its adherents are not intent on converting people. Conversion is not necessary. Witches live with tolerance and respect towards other spiritual paths. There is not one truth but many. A person who has had this experience of recognition will draw other Pagans and witches to them.

The images of orgies and naked covens which occur in the

media are grossly inaccurate. They bear no resemblance to rites within a witch's religion. Sex is accepted as part of nature by Pagan philosophy, but this just means that they do not condemn it between consenting adults of either or both sexes, in the way which most patriarchal religions do. Selina, for example, is not facilitating a coven at the moment, naked or otherwise. Instead she works alone or with her partner or informally as a High Priestess within the Pagan community in her locality. This position means she is called upon for spiritual counsel, to help train and develop others, to hear and hold rituals and to give magical advice and divination.

Witches do not sacrifice animals or people but make personal sacrifices as a way of symbolically letting go of an old influence in order to be ready for the new. For example, a Pagan who wishes for healing may sacrifice an unhealthy diet or a destructive habit like tobacco addiction. Spells are performed by witches but not in the fairy-tale manner, full of bats' wings and spiders' legs. These are remnants of herbal healing lore using folk names for plants from a time before doctors. Lizards' leg and eye of newt are examples of this nomenclature, referring metaphorically to certain herbs used in the cauldron ritual.

The 'magic' witches use involves ancient archetypes and symbols which give access to the unconscious and transform it, thus enabling Pagans to make conscious changes in their lives and in the lives of others. Spells work where there is need. The rules are that the magic must be sincere and the intent good. It must not harm or seek to control any other person, and witches must expect to have to answer to the Goddess three times. Magic is a word with connotations of trickery or malintent, but this is not possible or necessary within true Pagan codes of belief.

All this Selina has taught me. Most people envisage witches as wrinkled hags covered in boils dancing naked at midnight around a dead goat on a windy Cornish hill! So the last image they would conjure up is my sister - an attractive twenty-five-year-old woman casually stirring a cauldron in her back garden on a council estate in Bucks.

Selina has another sister with whom she has been reunited in this life. Her name is Suzy and she comes from Yorkshire, county of Mother Shipton, the great foreseer. We get along as well as three sisters should. Often we go shopping together in the West End. We like Top Shop. Sometimes at the end of a spree we go to our favourite restaurant in Crouch End. They do not have goat on the menu so we order feta cheese salad and drink Strega. I had better not give you the name of the restaurant in case the Witchfinder General decides to close it down.

I suppose there is still the occasional flash of sibling rivalry. I do envy Selina her absolute faith. Because I live in London, I cannot often make it to the festivals. While I spend October 31st watching a tacky re-run of *Halloween Part IV*, fending off local kids with fun size Mars bars, Selina spends her Samhain evening dancing with her broomstick and fellow Pagans, singing to the moon within a sacred stone circle. It is not just her faith that I envy, but more so her freedom to indulge in activities which as a child brought such pleasure. Sometimes at night, looking out at a full moon, I cannot help but think, maybe it is time to slip a silver pentacle around my neck and head for the hills.

Back on the Buckinghamshire step, watching my sister stirring and incanting, I realise I am not so much a part of it now. I can only sit and observe the ritual. I can no longer make it the centre of my life like Selina does. I may have traded my broomstick for a Fiat Panda (which I traded for the 127), but I still have Girolamo Savanorola, *La Strega*, the Black Eagle and the Evil Eye in my wardrobe. Perhaps my word processor is my cauldron, a vessel for my magic. And this is my spell.

SOPHIE HANNAH

MASKS

- 1 -

Who to impersonate today? Let's see.
Who states the obvious? It isn't me.

My name is Jesus. Crucifixion hurts.
My name is Scott. It's bloody cold outside.
Yves St. Laurent: I like designing shirts.
Guy Fawkes: my plan went wrong and then I died.

I am the stone inside the avocado.
I am a tight-arsed door to door bastardo.

- 2 -

The new arrivals cannot be ignored.
They look a bit like Bob and Charlie Ford.
I must protect my only wedded lord.

Preserve your mind - it's an elite hotel.
Stripsearch each passer-by who rings the bell.
I own some shares. I too have wares to sell.

Four years, four sodding years and nothing done.
I'm standing here, two for the price of one,
In mint condition. My idea of fun

Might be the same as yours. What would you miss?
Not conversation, and an orifice
Is, after all, only an orifice.

- 3 -

(One innuendo, everyone's excited.)
Call it a long shot, call it unrequited -
I'm only here because I was invited.

SOPHIE HANNAH

THE ZOO-KEEPER

I hear you've got yourself another ape
Without so much as asking my advice.
Which of us had the luckier escape?
Probably me. I keep myself in shape;
My life so far could be described as nice.

You'd change all that (I'm sure you know you would).
Don't come round here to buy your loaf of bread.
You'd rather be attacked than understood.
There's not a one of 'em that's any good,
As both Ed Begley and my grandma said.

I'm not quite sure whether I've won or lost.
I'm half-relieved, half-jealous and it's strange.
There's still a line that I have never crossed -
This is my fan club. Guess how much they cost -
Nor do I want my attitude to change

In any way. What are we going to do?
Nothing, of course. Tradition is tradition.
Could I be more traditional than you?
I feel like someone's auntie at the zoo
Or in the bloody jungle on a mission.

SOPHIE HANNAH

This is a slow and complicated game.
I like it, though, because it takes so long.
And if I die, please write beneath my name
She wanted everything to stay the same.
How can you ask? Of course there's something wrong.

FRED D'AGUIAR

TOWARDS HOME

Customs and Immigration

A MAN WALKS over a sheet of fibreglass sixty feet up, climbs through a window, trips a downstairs alarm and exits the way he came - through the window and over the fibreglass - without taking a penny with him. The house is his. He sleeps there nightly and calls out in his sleep. But to have told the truth to those close to him, that he was hungry or thirsty or dying for a pee and, in the process, tripped the alarm he forgot how to turn off, would have been worse somehow. To lie was easier. To cook up a burglary. To leave the entire family paranoid about a fortress' supposed impregnability. That house is England and I am a British Subject.

I have been away and I've forgotten the code that would open the doors to the fortress and let me breeze in. My clumsy return in a state of absentmindedness has triggered the biggest alarm of all - that I no longer belong. And there's no one to turn it off. The police show up with a barrage of questions. In this slanted light their faces are creased and their tone disbelieving, incredulous, ridiculing. I speak because I have a game to get through. If I don't play, then their questions will cease and I will be jailed for trying to enter the place - this country - illegally. So I go along with their sarcasm and disdain knowing that, however extreme their behaviour, there exists the final restraint of procedure - a number of bendable rules that are open to abuse (and often abused) but dependable too because there.

England, you continue to erect barriers against my entry and re-entry. Your fibreglass roof that doubles as my glass ceiling continues to offer meagre support. But one day, I know it will simply dissolve. For now, I traverse it with a burglar's aplomb by making myself lighter than my actual bodyweight, by lifting myself as I step on the balls of my feet, by never slouching or stepping onto my heels, by hardly breathing: by guile.

- 2 -

THE airplane has landed. A terminal building offers fresh, heated air compared with that breathed in the cabin of the jet. I think I'm here, home, back. But I am not. When I get to passport control I know that I am in a space that is nowhere: land and not land, England and somewhere in between the place I have left and my final destination. Suddenly everything about my arrival is predicated on the smooth passing of the moment. If I present my passport and there is a problem, I will not be let into the country - simple as that. This space, that nether world, increases my heart rate and causes my breathing to become rapid and shallow. I think they will find some fault with the 'British Citizen' stamp, some hitch in the photograph or details of my birth and residence.

It is not a rational feeling, nor is it explained away by attributing it to paranoia or a highly strung sensibility. The feeling of 'unbelongingness' is grounded in a reality comprised of years of detail: personal affronts, political betrayal, professional snobbery - all on the basis of my racial difference. Somehow this passport feels like a forgery. I think, 'My God, what if it has been revoked?!' I feel it is a privilege, not a right. I am able to breathe again and quiet my heart when I am waved through the narrow gate and the little book is handed back to me. I've made it. My cover - whatever it is - has not been blown.

- 3 -

BUT I know I can't breathe too easily. I should have nothing to worry about. My luggage is mine. Packed by me and free of contraband. Yet I am nervous as I straighten and walk through the 'nothing to declare' portion of Customs. Clearly I have plenty to declare. Without uttering a word I have declared my race, my generation, my sex. These categories place me within the most dangerous bracket of legal stereotypes - THE YOUNG BLACK MALE.

I can see from the looks that the customs officers throw my way that they are certain they will find something if they bother to stop me and unpack my bags. I shoot back a look of 'I am Mother Teresa heavily made up to look like a young black man.' But in my head I'm counting from one to ten, in my certainty that before I reach ten, one of these officers will approach me. 'Six', and my heel is caught by the trolley behind me pushed by a fool without a driving license. 'Seven'; but, I correct myself, even with a clean license - an advanced proficiency test to boot - it is impossible to drive one of these things. 'I forgive you', is the look I cast back to the person behind me. 'Eight'. My own trolley veers to the left and I pull hard on it - harder than I intended - swerving it to the left and speeding up for a few feet. 'Nine'. 'Excuse me, Sir. Where have you come from?' And I try hard not to look pissed off. I answer in my best English as taught to me by my excessively polite-to-strangers mother.

At least I am not searched, just asked a few searching questions. 'Was I on business or pleasure?' 'What's the nature of the business?' When I say I teach and what I teach I am allowed to go. This may seem like a standard exchange between a figure in authority - a kind of gatekeeper - and someone seeking permission to proceed, but it is more than that. The certainty that I will be stopped, and my doubts about my qualifications for entry, have been instilled over nearly two dozen years of residence. And that residence itself has been shaped by uncertainty about my status (examine the numerous changes to immigration law since 1972) and by hostility directed at my mind and body. (One instance was Margaret Thatcher's repeated use of the word 'swamp' whenever she referred to immigration, during her '79 election campaign. Her utterance legitimised this hostility and, by association, raised the spectre of Powell's 'rivers of blood'.)

- 4 -

I BREATHE again and run the gauntlet of fresh faces waiting for relatives and friends. One of those faces belongs to me. It always meets me on the other side. It has no memory of the hot flushes and cold sweats engendered by Passport Control and Customs. It has never left. A passing car has never slowed down to shout 'nigger' at this face. It has never been chased from a pub, or had to run into a yard to escape a mob, or turned up for a job sporting the wrong skin, or had the police punch it in the face regardless of a pair of Joe 90 Specs. This face has no memory and, therefore, all these negatives are lost to it. This face exists and will continue to greet me when I return from abroad. If one day it is not here in the crowd, smiling, waving and fresh, I'll know I've remembered too much, kept too much on file to be happy here. During the walk along that gangway of reception and exceptional friendship I put on that face, I belong.

-5-

THE two faces, one black, the other British, cannot be soldered together into Black-British. The hyphen - the bridge - will always be necessary. But it lacks the dignity and implied heritage of the double-barrel hyphenated name so many single Englishmen and women in their thirties seem to brandish. 'Black-British' wears its hyphen like a plaster. There to keep some wound from further haemorrhaging and exposure; and proving inadequate for both. The hyphen ensures that the two words never unite. It serves as a reminder of their difference. The Black- (for hyphen read 'not') British are a separate species, an adjunct. This hyphen joins but is

highly visible as a reminder of that join, that potential for severance.
Therefore, Black-British I am not. British, yes. Black, indisputably. But no hyphen, please. The hyphen becomes a 'v'. (Harrison's 'V' for 'versus' and 'fuck off') and Black can never win that fight. Black becomes the fall guy; the one who must dive without dignity or honour to the canvas at the allotted time for an inferior purse. The hyphen is an automatic assault on the 'Black', an automatic ennobler and enabler of the British that precedes it, a subjugator of the black, knee-capping its potential for power and independence by colonising it all over again. To say I am 'black this' or 'black that', is to qualify my endeavour with a term that is too general, too susceptible to highjack by one group or other to be of any use to me.

My Britishness goes so far back, and is so intertwined with what it means to live as a citizen in the UK, that any discussion of 'blackness' - or the hyphenated nature of belonging to an unwelcoming, excluding, tribalised, class-infected, democratic-authoritarian, race-caste, place - automatically becomes a discussion of the central facts of that place. To avoid sounding needlessly defensive, I should say that the terms 'blackness' and 'Britishness' revise themselves to the point where platitudes must be discarded, so that an examination of the UK can occur.

Britain, the word, the idea, the reality, engenders so much venom that the act of embracing Britishness is tantamount to cuddling a scorpion. I don't mind grappling with a complex history. Worse would be to have no history. Historylessness is in that hyphen. Without it I'd be lost in a general term: 'black'. With it, I am condemned to second-class citizenship. So ditch the hyphen, and the qualifier, and keep the 'British'. Confound all those who feel they can advocate that term after slavery, colonialism, imperialism and multi-national corporate-run economies. Such deadening words as these inform the sophistication and sophistry of Britishness. I want to be a part of that trickiness. I want to feel the burglar in his own home for as long as I am able to let the household know how I feel, and so long as I am not denied entry, on the basis of skin pigmentation of all things, for Christ's sake!

-6-

AT THE airport, on my return, I should be able to greet that optimistic aspect of myself with open arms, knowing full well that forgetting my hurts is part of being able to still belong (even if 'still belong' sounds like 'still born').

I don't know of a single soul who has thrived on envy and anger without that soul shrivelling to nothing. I have met many shrivelled souls. Their catalogue of grievances is all too real, but so often rehearsed as to take the place of life itself, and of the potential for life, and of the chance to find love as a substitute for grief. I celebrate the light and landscape, the city and the arts, and some of the people of this island, as I invoke the word home. As I do so, I feel at the same time the threat of the scorpion and the comfort of touching a child's hair or of holding a new book. The word 'home' must retain its duplicity, its Anancy trickster self.

'Towards home' still leaves me homeless, homing, ill at ease with what I possess of the noun, and therefore investing it with verbal qualities to capture its sense of unsettledness, upheaval. It is as if I've made that airport terminal my home and I'm doomed to be forever arriving at Passport Control and Customs as a necessary condition of belonging. The aspect of myself that greets me every time - and is forever forgetful of the last ugly time - makes each arrival new; this time, maybe, the awful expectations will not be fulfilled. This is how I am able to return. This is why when I am greeted by someone who is me and who has never left, the 'I' that has just seen enough to turn back, continues onwards, blends with the other waiting, renewing, self, and is renewed in turn.

Home is not about arriving at a place, but travelling towards it; a myth. The ideal space for understanding this ungraspable thing is at an airport. But I have had to belong somewhere, in the first instance, however ambivalently, in order to continue to feed this lucrative myth of unbelonging.

This sounds miles away from the sticks and stones reality of, say, Tower Hamlets in East London, and may be something of a privileged, and, by extension, irrelevant discourse. But I am also dealing with the terrain of name-calling (by the way, that maxim is false - negative names do exact a toll, if they are shouted loud enough and long enough) where the bad names become internalised and must be extirpated if the afflicted subject is to function through acts of forgetting that are tantamount to forgiving.

I must forget the calumnies and canards concerning my skin (to list them here would give them the very legitimacy I seek to deny them) that convert speech acts to acts of violence and institutionalised racism, if I am to be met at the airport by that part of me still capable of love.

LES MURRAY

CONTESTED LANDSCAPE AT FORSAYTH

The conquest of fire-culture
on that timber countryside
has broadcast innumerable
termite mounds all through
the gravel goldrush hills
and the remnant railhead town,
petrified French mustards
out of jars long smashed.

Train platform and tin Shire
are beleaguered in nameless cemetery.
Outworks of the Dividing range
are annulled under Dreaming-turds.
It's as if every place a miner
cursed, or thought of sex,
had its abraded marker. Mile
on mile of freckled shade,
the ordinary is riddled by
cylinder-pins of unheard music.

LES MURRAY

On depopulated country
frail billions are alive
in layered earthen lace.
Their every flight is
a generation, gluing towers
which scatter and mass
on a blind smell-plan.
Cobras and meta-cobras
in the bush, immense black vines
await monsoon in a world
of clay lingam altars.

Like the monuments to every
mortal thing that a planet without God
would require, and inscriptionless
as rage would soon weather those,
the anthills erupt on verges,
on streets, round the glaring pub,
its mango tree and sleeping-fridges,
an estuary of undergrounds,
khaki prunts on dusty glass.

RUTH PADEL

TELL ME ABOUT IT

When they mourn you over there
the way you'd want, the way you mourn
your friends; when they're celebrating

having loved you in Derry, Rathmullen,
wherever - birettas, candles, Latin,
all the weavings you don't believe in

but love anyway and I'll never share
for who the hell converts to ex-Catholic? -
no one will know someone's missing you here

for ever. Whose arms, printed with
that absolute man's stillness
when your breath calms

into my shoulder and you fall asleep
inside me, open and close
in a foreign night round nothing.

Who misses the way
you pour loose change on the bar
in a puddle of fairy-tale silver

and move through the night, through
everything, curious, mischievous as
a mongoose, and never an unkind word.

I might dream of coming over. Touching
just one friend's sleeve. To whisper
'Talk about him. A bit. The way he was,

here', but never do it. Instead I'll say *Yes*
in my sleep to you. To no one.
You'll put your tongue in my mouth,

deep, the way you do, and my eyes will open
on a dark garden. I'll wake up
touching myself for you. The alarm

will stare witch-green digits. I'll hang on
to the fragile haze of a winebar
when you leant over the foreign formica,

haltering my hand within your two
like the filling in a sandwich,
sashaying the skin of each finger

down to the soft web between,
over and over, a rosary of rub
and slide, as if you could solder

me to your lifeline. As if
you could take me with you.
And I'll wish you had.

PAUL EUSTICE

SIX EGGS

To write, to make black marks upon the white, is to discover. To discover that and to discover unto. To find out, show, disclose, perceive, facilitate perception. Today I have some words to write, record, to mould, to click together and to live in. But where to begin?

D ID I ever tell you about Old Charlotte? Ninety she is, and lives two doors away. We lived mere neighbours for several years, saying 'good morning' as I passed the gate, and then I was ill. She brought me six eggs. To build me up, she said. She said she had a nephew with a similar complaint and this was accepted as an explanation. Next week she brought me six more. Large, free-range eggs in a box secured with an elastic band. It took her five minutes to negotiate the steps and passageway and soon I was in the habit of going to see her every Saturday morning. Once, I didn't go in and she came to the door when we were in bed on a Sunday morning. She hammered on the door with her stick and said 'You didn't collect yer eggs so I brung 'em round'. Trapped in my own burrow.

So what about this old lady? A record of her past, her conversation? Perhaps.

PAUL EUSTICE

To avoid the enemy of a Sunday morning, the best defence is attack on a Saturday. Before lunch, that gets it out of the way. And not immediately before lunch, or the smell decreases appetite. Oh yes, she smells on occasion. She also laughs quite often and has amused me in several ways. Subtle, her bait. We established the habit of a few words over the eggs. They might not appear until we'd clocked up half an hour of conversation and if I didn't collect them they'd be delivered. Whether I wanted them or not. Sometimes there was money in the box. That was embarrassing because she had very little and I have enough, but she is obstinate. It is her obstinacy that keeps her going, digging the garden with a spade in one hand and a stick in the other, living alone and in good humour. Well, usually in good humour.

The smell is complex. I once wrote to a friend that I would carry out a chemical analysis of her aroma in the interests of science. I said I would register a claim for the rich vein of mineral deposits dormant in the folds of her neck. Was that cruel? I don't think so.

The front room of her lair, whatever uncertain purpose it serves, is infested with flies all summer and with damp musty smells all winter. The back room smells of pig's trotters in soak, burned remains on the gas stove and rotted remains in little crevices. It smells of the large tin bath full of sand, which is apparently for the cat to pee in, and of the old stove which is always surrounded with raked ashes.

She keeps her dandelion wine under the table because she has forgotten the next stage of the recipe. It is next to the paraffin for the fire and a shovel, and candles, and copies of *The Daily Express* which she offers me from time to time. She has a gramophone with a handle and some old 78s. Last year she played me one and, as she held the table, she swayed in what was supposed to be time with the music. That was a high point in our relationship, intimacy and trust.

I don't think the cat ever does pee in the tin bath. For one thing, it's too high and exposed to view. For another, it has a large garden to do it in. But it does spend a lot of time indoors. She worries, you see, and occasionally panics. I often hear her in the garden, calling for her cat in a raucous voice that carries for miles and frightens the crows.

'Tommy Tommy. Here Tommy. Quick, quick. Fish. Tommytommytommy. Fishfishfish.'

I laugh when I hear that cry. If I visit her when Tommy is not responding, I have to help round him up, otherwise she troubles me with her concern for him. He bites her, sometimes, but then he has liver trouble and is excusably irritable when disturbed yet again just to put her mind at rest. She wraps the bite in a dirty old bandage and she survives. Probably immune, or perhaps the aromatic cloud around her acts as a sort of general antidote to lesser sources of infection. It is certainly strong. Once, I was in there and her friend Jessie arrived. That seemed to confuse and embarrass her and she wet herself. I had to go to a corner and retch, hoping she wouldn't notice. I'm sure she didn't.

I could dwell for hours on the physical details of her little world. The photographs of herself at twenty-three and of a gravestone; the religious paintings on the brown and yellow walls; her father's tools in an old wooden chest and the police whistle she wears round her neck. Her father was a chimney sweep and she wants to brush her own chimney once more before she dies. I laughed when she told me that, and she shared the joke. But she will try it nevertheless.

> Am I expiating guilt? Forgive me father, tap tap tap, for I have been callous. No, I feel quite virtuous about the length and regularity of my visits, even though (because?) I sometimes resent them. Shall I retell her narrative? Shall I record it unvarnished or invent around it? I am using her without her knowledge. Or is she using me - taking me over again in the intimacy of my own study?

Her narrative grew piecemeal out of our lengthening conversation. It was difficult to listen to and impossible to repeat. She is clinically insane. At least, she is sometimes. Other times she is shrewd and penetrating - when she isn't overtired, or worried, and she hasn't read the paper. The newspaper is the worst source of confusion. She reads the headlines and believes it is all happening around her. BABY DIES. Is it the baby next door? Have I seen it lately and can I reassure her it hasn't gone? I can usually tell the newspaper news; it sounds so unlikely for our little group of dwellings. But I have no end of trouble in persuading her it has nothing to do with us. Ask not for whom the bell tolls, it was someone in Dagenham and you haven't been there.

Most of the time I say very little. My function is to listen, and sometimes to reassure her so I don't have to listen to unwonted fears, which are irritating. I prefer to listen to her tales of the past and her analysis of the present, because there is material there for the game of 'construct your neighbour'. I can construct her in the image I choose from the hints she throws out, and sometimes I think my image is near the truth. I can't confirm this, of course, as nobody knows the truth. Her nephew knows a little of it, but he stays away. Anyway, her narrative begins with her grandfather.

He was a rag-and-bone man and she used to help him sort the rags. Piecing together the separate half-hours with their variations on a theme, I have a narrative which proceeds from here to her late teens. At that point in the story she is working with some old ladies, pushing their bath chairs around the sea-front. Enter a man, son of a wealthy farmer and father of illegitimate children beyond number.

'He was a bad 'un, you know, but he couldn't 'elp it. It was in 'is nature - you can't 'elp what's in yer nature.'

He wanted his wicked way with her, but he couldn't get it. I suppose that was in her nature. She had a strict Baptist upbringing which sometimes sits awkwardly with her rustic humour but has left its mark on her conversation. (She once found a frozen chicken on her doorstep, from an anonymous well-wisher. 'God works in a mysterious way and 'e sent me down a chicken', was her grateful comment.) She told him (the bad 'un), as she often reminds me, 'I wouldn't leave those old people, not fer anything.' Whatever that meant, she evidently thinks it was her refusal of a wicked, if possibly tempting offer. He told his father and his father said 'Give her the money anyway'. So she tells me, and the amount is elaborated from £300 to £300,000 to £300 million. With this she built a hospital and in the hospital occurs the first of her anecdotes.

A husband and wife from her church were admitted at the same time, accompanied on their arrival by her friend Jessie. The matron insisted they go to separate wards but Jessie declared 'Whom God hath joined, let no man put asunder'. And so they were put in the same bed.

I think it was about this time she met the gipsy. He was hired - I forget by whom - to do her a mischief of some sort. I'm not sure what sort, but she claimed she was hit on the head with an axe in her youth and this has split her brain in two to make her twice as clever as anyone else. The cat bears the scars of this wound for her. (Her cat is as old as she is and they were both born blind, receiving their sight when she fell over and hit her head on the pavement. Perhaps all this is connected.) The gipsy fell in love with her and so she escaped unharmed.

She didn't marry him - she's a spinster - and she never did say how their love blossomed. Probably it didn't, but I suspect she was a very romantic child.

We move on from there to when she brought a farm. She also bought and built most of the town we live in, along with several other buildings, but the town has forgotten the fact, she says. She gave the farm to her cousin to run but he spent the income on high living and let it decay. There is a lot of jealousy in her family and this is also connected, on alternate Saturdays. Then she came down here, when all the roads were fields, and had her uncle and aunt to stay. She went upstairs recently to take them their tea - a tray with a dirty old cloth, two cups and saucers, cucumber sandwiches and the best sugar bowl. She got halfway up the stairs and remembered they died in 1946.

She thought it was funny.

So did I, at the time.

> I still do. Many of her stories are amusing, bitter-sweet. Like the one about her nephew's wife. She had written to say she could not come to pay a long-awaited visit because she was strapped to a board on account of her bad back. The old lady spent many happy hours reminding Tommy and I that the invalid was supposed to be a faith healer, and cackling 'physician heal thyself'.
> But did she believe the excuse?

I do not think so. I am too afraid of her intelligence to be condescending. Finding herself amusing, does she find others transparent in her moments of clarity? When her anecdotes are probed for motive - for the membrance and the telling of them - what is revealed of her machinations? What kind of woman is growing old in that smelly frame? What is the experience doing to her? (I assume, of course, I reconstruct her accurately, without undue distortion through my own murky corners.) I want to know what kind of middle age she had. In the tattered frame are the remnants of a life, a history of motivation. I want to know how much she understands, controls.

I want to know why she gave me the eggs.

There is much more to her narrative, but I don't know how to make sense of it all. Some of it is clearly part of her lunacy. The avowed fact, for example, that she was born Florence Nightingale. Perhaps she meant she was born in her time. Or perhaps it is her way of saying how virtuous she was in building the hospital. It's the sort of thought she might have. She claims she was born Harry Bell. Born as him, with him, for him, because of him? She was born the Blue Queen. There is a sundial in the sky. There is a Stone Man. I am the Stone Man, some Saturdays. On other days I am merely presumed to know all about it. She thinks I know all about everything - the names and places of her past, the events she refers to in passing. I understand all that, according to her, and am obviously the sole confidant on such important matters. Or so she would have me believe.

I seem to be part of a conspiracy of hers to meet the world with a smile and then discuss it with jovial scepticism when it isn't looking. Like Jessie, for example. Jessie comes to visit her friend when her migraine allows and it isn't raining. And when she can afford the bus fare. When she has gone, to wait for a bus in the cold south-westerly, her friend tells me she is a well-meaning nuisance. Sometimes she is said to be jealous of something undefined. Maybe so.

Is her continuance of the narrative and the flow of anecdote the purpose of trapping me in there every week? Or is it a means to forge a closer bond, involving me more closely in her existence? The eggs lead to the stories, the stories lead to... to what? A little gardening, pruning her tree a few weeks ago. This is part of our relationship, but whether part of its purpose or of its method I cannot tell. Perhaps it is just a by-product.

Why does she constantly refer to her imaginary wealth? To explain the jealousy she refers to? Or to imply, as she quite plainly stated recently, that she is able to reward those who assist her. After the eggs, the coins in the box, the legacy. It's an ugly possibility, to pass as rich in order to buy company on credit. If it were a consequence of desperate loneliness it would be natural to feel pity. If it is a measure of the way her mind has always worked, it may explain her loneliness, and may increase it. Perhaps it is a measure of what she thinks of me, and my possible motives.

That is what the whole question boils down to. Is an old lady entrapping me with her eggs and her age and her stories because she is lonely, or is she lonely because she has spent much of her life entrapping people with eggs and coins, an aura of wealth, or a smile that promised more than it meant to yield? Did she embarrass her nephew away with the legacy ploy?

How am I to judge this woman whom I have possibly created? And what am I to say about our relationship, what learn from it as I record this version? Who am I to judge? Creator, victim, friend? She will continue to spread her net until she rots beyond repair into a corner of her weedy garden and Tommy and I are left in peace. And then I shall probably reconstruct her as a fascinating character I used to know, an amiable independent old girl with a secret past and a rustic guile which enabled her to see through the outer layers of her visitors.

> For this task I shall adopt a persona. And I shall treat it as a work of fiction. That is her legacy to me. A life which can drain into orderly black marks, and so anaesthetise myself against the memory.

When the sores on her legs were discovered it was decided she would have to go to hospital. She died on the second day away from home. Tommy is put down. Her chimney, unswept, is being removed as her nephew renovates his inheritance. I never wish to read these words again. Except, perhaps, to correct the spelling.

BACK NUMBERS

ISSUE A
The Devil interviews Douglas Dunn, a previously undiscovered short story by Patrick Hamilton, and an essay by his biographer Nigel Jones, John Williams' prison journals, stories by Suzannah Dunn and Sue Roe, poems by Don Paterson, Eva Salzman, Laurence Lerner, Jonathan Taylor, Caroline Price and Hubert Moore. £3.95

ISSUE B
The Devil interviews Simon Raven, six poems from Matthew Sweeney, a biographical essay on Jocelyn Brooke by David Kennedy, Terry James' autobiopic, prose poems from John Burnside, Martyn Ford's Bibliophiles, stories from Mark Illis, Stephen Ormsby, Nicky Singer and Helen Slavin, poems by Ian Caws, Elizabeth James and David Kennedy. £ 3.95

ISSUE C
Film number. The Devil interviews Christopher Hampton. Hugo Williams on Sex in the Cinema. Roy Apps on the origins of the British Film Industry. Stuart Hood on Pasolini's Theorem. Fiction from Christina Prado and Margaret Wilkinson. Poetry from Ian Duhig, Helen Dunmore, Kathleen Jamie, Robert Crawford and George Charlton. Plus Felix Salten the pornographer who wrote Bambi, and Jimmy Hoffa. £3.95

ISSUE D
Satire issue. The Devil's Audience with Alasdair Gray, Seamus Heaney's translation of The Midnight Verdict, A.L. Kennedy's emotional moles, dystopias of Scott Bradfield and Christopher Hope, Amy Friedman on women's satire, W.N. Herbert on Scottish satire, Peter Porter's Verse versus Politics. In The Devil's Confessional: Vicki Feaver, Gregory Woods, Hugo Williams, Judith Kazantzis. The Devil's Sermon on Railways. Reviews of Dirk Bogarde, John Guare and Neil Corcoran. £4.99

NEW NUMBERS

ISSUE F

to appear spring/summer 1995 will be THE DEVIL'S LEGAL ISSUE. Deadly Sin: Sloth. We will publish the best Anthems of the Republic in this issue. We are also pleased to receive tracts. Contributions are invited accompanied by sae.

Future subscribers will receive automatic membership of The Society for the Suppression of Virtue. The offer, like virginity, lasts for a limited period only.

Single copies and subscriptions available from:

THE PRINTER'S DEVIL
Top Offices,
13a Western Road,
Hove, East Sussex, BN3 1AE.
Telephone 0273 720894

CONTRIBUTORS' NOTES

NICK HORNBY'S novel *High Fidelity* will be published in March by Victor Gollancz. He is currently working on a film script of *Fever Pitch*.

KEN SMITH'S most recent collection of poetry is *Tender to the Queen of Spain*, published by Bloodaxe Books. He co-edited the Anthology *Klaonica: Poems from Bosnia* published in 1993 by Bloodaxe.

SOPHIE HANNAH lives in Manchester. She has published two pamphlets of poetry. Her first full-length collection, *The Hero and the Girl Next Door*, is due from Carcanet in 1995.

U. A. FANTHORPE'S *Selected Poems* was published by Penguin in 1986. She won an Arts Council Writer's Award in 1994. Her next collection is due to appear in Spring 1995.

CAROLE COATES' poetry has appeared in *Outposts*, *The Rialto* and other magazines. A college lecturer, she has published articles and criticism, including a study of the novelist John Cowper Powys. She is currently working on a novel.

MICHAEL DONAGHY is an American poet who lives in England. His first book *Shibboleth* earned him the Geoffrey Faber Memorial Award. His latest collection of poems is *Errata*. (Oxford University Press).

RUTH PADEL'S latest collection, *Angel* (Bloodaxe 1993) was a Poetry Book Society Recommendation. Her next prose book, *Whom the Gods Destroy*, comes out in March.

LES MURRAY was born in 1938 in New South Wales. His *Collected Poems* and book of essays *The Paperback Tree* were published by Carcanet His most recent collection of poems is *Translations from the Natural World*.

FRED D'AGUIAR grew up in Guyana. He is the author of three books of poems, the most recent of which is *British Subjects*, published by Bloodaxe. His first novel *The Longest Memory* appeared from Chatto and Windus in 1994.

ALISON SPRITZLER-ROSE'S poetry has appeared in *The Observer*. An American, she has lived in this country for eight years. She is finishing her first novel.

EMILIA DI GIROLAMO lives in London where she works as an actress. She lectures at Middlesex University and is currently writing a PhD on drama in prisons. Her play *Committed* will be produced by Too Far Out Theatre Co. in September 1995.

PAUL EUSTICE lives in Worthing and is Head of Media and Photography at Brighton College of Technology.

SEAN O'BRIEN'S most recent book of poems is *HMS Glasshouse* (Oxford University Press). A collection of essays titled *The Deregulated Muse* is to be published by Bloodaxe.

STEPHEN PLAICE is currently writing for *The Bill*. Two plays, *Boleyn* and *Britannia* will go into production in 1995.

FIACHRA GIBBONS works for *The Guardian* and for *The Independent on Sunday*. He was born in Ireland.

EVA SALZMAN'S book of poems *The English Earthquake* is published by Bloodaxe. She reviews for *The Independent* and has recently finished a screenplay.